CALL ME TRUE

CALL ME TRUE

A Biography of True Davidson

ELEANOR DARKE

NATURAL HERITAGE/NATURAL HISTORY INC.

Published by Natural Heritage/Natural History Inc.
P.O. Box 95, Station O, Toronto, Ontario M4A 2M8

First Edition

Canadian Cataloguing in Publication Data

Darke, Eleanor
    Call Me True

Includes bibliographical references and index.
ISBN 1-896219-34-9

1. Davidson, True, 1901–1978. 2. Women Politicians -
Ontario - East York-Biography. 3. Politicians - Ontario -
East York-Biography. 4. East York (Ont.) - Biography.
I. Title.

FC3099.E36Z49 1997   971.3'54104'092   C97-931447-X
F1059.5.E23D37 1997

Cover and book design by Norton Hamill Design
Cover photo Circa 1970. *Ashley and Crippen*
Back cover photo of True Davidson, 1922, Strasbourg, Saskatchewan, where she later recalled that she "taught English, History, Science and Art in all collegiate grades and was principal of a 3-room High School and a 5-room Public School." She was then 21 years old. *Courtesy David Cobden.*

THE CANADA COUNCIL | LE CONSEIL DES ARTS
FOR THE ARTS | DU CANADA
SINCE 1957 | DEPUIS 1957

Natural Heritage/Natural History Inc. acknowledges the support received for its publishing program from the Canada Council Block Grant Program. We also acknowledge with gratitude the assistance of the Association for the Export of Canadian Books, Ottawa.

PRINTED AND BOUND IN CANADA BY HIGNELL PRINTING, WINNIPEG, MANITOBA

CONTENTS

CALL ME TRUE

INTRODUCTION

"Just call me True," she'd say when being introduced. She didn't like being called "Miss Davidson"; despised "Ms"; and, much as she gloried in her position as Mayor of East York, was politically astute enough to avoid the over-use of her title. Throughout her political career, she used the name "True" to define her character, policies and beliefs. But what can we "truly" say about True? In 1968, she told a reporter that "life in politics is like living in a goldfish bowl and the refractions mask what you really are. You have to let people think as they like and you go ahead and be as you are. If you have great luck and good friends you are successful. My life is an open book and sometimes I think it's a cartoon."[1]

Her opponents would laugh at the supposed passivity of this statement, arguing that True never missed an opportunity to use the media to present her own image of herself. If she was a goldfish, she was one with a doctorate in the control of refractions. She told the same stories of her life repeatedly, carefully revealing only what she wanted while ensuring that the reporter got enough material not to feel the need to dig for more. She was content to be painted as a cartoon. It was politically effective and ensured some personal privacy. Cartoons, after all, communicate their message simply and clearly and are more quickly understood than a fully detailed drawing.

True was a complex personality; frequently contradictory in her opinions; changing opinions (and her vote) repeatedly on many issues. She could be irascible, demanding, opinionated and caustic, yet she was often kindly and she was always dedicated and deeply devoted to the people of "her" municipality. I hope that the reader of this book will find in it a more fully-fleshed True than the cartoon she projected to the newspapers, although I doubt whether anyone could capture all of her variations.

As she told *Star* reporter, Brian Swarbrick, in 1971, "There are various aspects of truth. What seems true when reviewing one aspect may not necessarily be true when considering another ..."[2]

This book and my search for the "true True" would never have happened without help from a long list of people. I never would have begun it without the encouragement and support of John Ridout, Chair of the East York Historical Society and of my publisher, Barry Penhale, of Natural Heritage Books. True would have approved of John and Barry's efforts; as she told the Barrie Kiwanis Club in 1928, "anyone who did anything to promote Canadian literature was doing a service to his country."[3]

The staff at Victoria College and the Metropolitan Toronto Reference Library were very helpful. Special thanks are due to the staff of the Archives and Special Collections section of the York University Archives who helped me work through the large collection of True's papers that were donated to them after her death. True was a pack-rat who didn't believe in wasting paper, frequently reusing the back of older documents and writings. Their patience and encouragement as I tried to sort out what was written when was very helpful. Since I did the research for this book while holding a full-time job, I am particularly appreciative of their willingness to try and work around my days off.

The written sources gave me the majority of the dates and events of her life but only a small taste of her personality. Fortunately, no one who met True ever forgot her and one of the great privileges I have had while working on this project has been the pleasure of meeting and speaking with some of the extraordinary people whom she knew. In fact, one of the most difficult parts of researching this book was deciding to stop interviewing. Every person I spoke to suggested at least two more people to whom "I had to speak." It was hard to declare a halt. Meeting such fascinating people enriched me as much as they did the book.

I am especially grateful to her nephews, David and Michael Cobden, for all of their help and advice. While the list of the others who shared their memories of her with me in interviews and letters is too long to provide here, I hope they will recognize their contributions in the text and accept my sincere appreciation for their help and honesty. If this book succeeds in any way to effectively convey a true picture of True, it will have been because of the memories and opinions that they so generously shared with me.

Eleanor Darke, 1997

1

A CHILD OF CANADA

FAMILY

Jean Gertrude Davidson was born in 1901 in Hudson, Quebec. She assumed the nickname, True, early and reinforced its use throughout her life, even refusing to acknowledge any other name on occasion[4]. Although the reference letters from her professors all called her Jean Gertrude[5], her listing in *Torontoniensis*, the University of Toronto yearbook listed her as J.G. "True" Davidson.[6] The first letter she received from Bryn Mawr offering her a scholarship addressed her as Miss J.G. Davidson, but subsequent letters were addressed to "True" Davidson, no doubt at her insistence.[7] Although she couldn't have known how useful it would be to her future career, her choice of name was an inspired one. As one of her friends later said, "It was a good name for her... she was smart...a good short political name."[8]

Because her father was a Methodist minister, the family moved frequently. By the time True left high school she had moved nine times and had lived in four different provinces. Although it was common for the Methodist clergy to change churches frequently, moves were generally within the same or nearby conferences. Her father appears to have difficulties as a minister, necessitating more frequent, complete changes. Charlotte Maher, who knew True near the end of her life, recalled her saying that her father "sort of got fired from some of his parishes."

True, herself, chose to regard these moves as a positive thing. As early as 1931, she was quoted as claiming "Canada in general as her home, for, she explained, she had lived in almost every province."[9]

True was enormously influenced by her father. She seems to have spent her whole life trying to live up to what she thought he wanted her to be, writing years later that:

> ...at school I was expected to top my class, and school, and even my province. Every time I met an expectation it became harder to face the next time I failed to do so...But it was not until I was a middle-aged woman and my father was dying that I discovered that he had been fiercely proud of me all along, and only wanted me to be all that I was capable of being. Which is very different from being first. And the realization changed my entire life...[10]

True's father, John Wilson Davidson. Reputedly a brilliant scholar, True's father seemingly lacked the interpersonal skills to be a successful minister. *Courtesy David Cobden*

True's father, John Wilson Davidson, was born at Union, Ontario, on April 29, 1870, one the large family of James Davidson and Jane Hepburn Grant, who was descended from the same ancestor as Ulysses S. Grant. True later described her ancestors as United Empire Loyalists, "the stiff-necked, unreasonable kind."[11] Like another famous woman of her generation, Agnes MacPhail, this family background had a marked influence on her personality. Terry Crowley wrote of the MacPhail's family that "More than their heritage made [them] hard-working and self-reliant. Life provided few cushions apart from the support of relatives, and they were only to be called upon in the most dire emergency."[12]

John Davidson's early education was in Union and St. Lambert, Ontario, and at the St. Thomas Collegiate Institute. He graduated in Arts from Victoria College in 1898 and then in Theology in 1900, winning numerous medals and prizes including the oratory prize. He was ordained the same year and immediately married Mary Elfleda Pomeroy, the daughter of a Methodist minister. Their first charge was the mission church at Hudson-on-the-Lake, Quebec, where True was born one year later. The next year they moved to St. Lambert, Quebec for one year; then to Montreal, where True's sister, Marsh, was born. These charges were followed in quick succession by Ormstown, Quebec (1904-5), Waterloo, Quebec (1905-9), and Delta, Ontario (1909-10). Then, when True was nine years old, they moved west to Vancouver (1913-1915), followed by a move to Regina where the pace of moves finally began to slow. Rev. Davidson served as minister of Wesley Church in Regina, Saskatchewn from 1915-1919; then moved to Rae Street Church, still in Regina, from 1919-22.[13]

The most open interview True ever gave about herself was to Warren Gerard for *The Globe Magazine* in 1971. In it she revealed an "extraordinary affection for her parents" and said of her father that:

> Well, he was a very brilliant man. The whole family was brilliant. They were of Scottish extraction...[She describes her father as not a worldly success in the church.] I don't know what happened. I think that perhaps my mother cared too much. Perhaps she was too ambitious for him. Perhaps he was too proud. Perhaps he had difficulty finding his way with people.[14]

True dedicated her book, *The Golden Strings*, to her father with a poem which reads in part:

To My Father

Misunderstood and lonely
Almost to the end,
Your courage never faltered,
Your will knew not to bend.

Pity you learned and patience
Beyond all grief or mirth,

And your love was rooted deeply
As a tree in ancient earth

You found a sweet solution
For frustrate human pain,
And your faith was clean and quiet
As grass after rain

She ends the poem with the dedication, "All I have done, my father, Since then, I owe to you."[15]

Whatever her father may have lacked in worldly abilities, True believed that he had a true calling and never doubted the sincerity of his faith. Her entire life appears to have been a search for the same depth of faith and for a calling to which she could give the same level of devotion. She told an interviewer that "I have a very clear recollection of church services. My father's hair became white very early and he did have a very rapt and dedicated look."[16] Although her religious faith was never as easy or uncomplicated as that her parents appear to have had, she credited them for having shared their faith with her and wrote that "My parents and my church may not have been, as they seemed to me, the best parents and best church in the world, but they gave me the God that I shall never quite lose. The best Christmas gift for any child."[17]

Charlotte Maher said that she always pictured True's father from her description as having been "a dour type who always dressed publicly in a tight collar..." All sources seem to indicate that he was an austere, very correct, highly intelligent, very principled man with a deep sense of religious calling, a scholar whose ascetic, reasoned faith wasn't easily conveyable to ordinary, compromising people.

In 1930, True wrote a short story which may have illustrated her belief that her father had sacrificed a successful scholarly career to work as a country minister. In the story, a country minister has written a novel and is considering submitting it for publication. His wife encourages him by reminding him of the kind comments made by his university professors about his writing. However the manuscript is unpublishable and the story ends with him having received a rejection letter from the publisher.

He turned to go, moving slowly and carefully like one in a dream. Five years' work gone for nothing—five years, and failure at the end! When they had all told him he could write!...He had been so sure he could write. The college magazine—all his professors—what had happened to him? Perhaps, after all, he was not the old Samson—not the old Samson, but Samson shorn, blinded and among his enemies. Perhaps, after all, more relentless than captivity or death, the years did something to a man. The years—the Philistine years.[18]

The same story portrayed a devotion between the minister and his wife that I would like to think was enjoyed by True's parents. "They looked at each other, and in their eyes again for a moment flared the gleam that age...cannot dim, and that is sweeter than many apple-blossoms."[19]

True's attachment to her mother wasn't as intense as the unity she felt with her father, although she respected her mother, saying of her that: "They [my parents] had a passion for truth and scholarship, and my mother had a passion for the arts as well. My mother painted. Our home was full of paintings when I was young. She was a musician. She was talented dramatically. She was the life of the church cultural programme."[20]

It appears that True's mother was devoted to her husband, but frustrated at his lack of success; a frustration likely deepened by comparison with her father's prominence within the church and by the fact that her success was totally dependent on that of her hus-

True's mother, Mary Elfleda [Pomeroy] Davidson. True loved her mother and cared for her for many years but was never as close to her as she was to her father. *Courtesy David Cobden*

True and her sister, Marsh. Even then True preferred to read a book! *Courtesy Michael Cobden*

band. While her father, Rev. John C. Pomeroy, also had been a scholar he had been a highly successful minister as well, holding several of the most important circuits and stations in the Methodist Church. He was described as being "highly gifted and...warm, impassioned and convincing...He possessed the most pleasing personality, his disposition being most kindly. It was easy for him to make friends. He was the life of any circle in which he found himself."[21]

Both of True's parents were very interested in the youth of the church. Their activities in this regard again illustrate the differences in their personalities. While True's father did committee work as Secretary of the Religious Education Committee of the Saskatchewan Conference, his wife was active in the creation of the Y.W.C.A. and in helping to organize the new Canadian Girls in Training (C.G.I.T.) group in their area.

The relationship between True and her sister, Marsh, was the most complex of all. True's nephew, Michael Cobden, later described it to Charlotte Maher, as "the original love-hate relationship." To me he said that his mother had been "the pretty one, the popular one" and that he had been astonished by the depth of resentment and rivalry that True later had expressed to him about his mother.[22] Marsh seems to have inherited all of their mother's social abilities and ease with people. The rivalry was primarily on True's side, caused by her insecurity regarding Marsh's popularity. She saw her sister as a rival for their parents' love. Charlotte Maher told me that she always felt that True "would have liked to have been like Marsh. I think she was envious of Marsh. I think she would have liked to have been little, and feminine and pretty."

Doris Tucker, who was Clerk of East York while True was Mayor and who shared many conversations with her, agreed that True had expressed resentment concerning her sister, feeling that she had been stuck with all the responsibility for the parents when they became old and that Marsh had an easier time in life than True. Doris particularly remembered that "her sister didn't go through what she went through to go to school. They were a little better off when the sister came along. She told me that."[23] True likely was referring here to the fact that she had to work for a few years between taking her B.A. and her

True and her sister Marsh as children. *Courtesy David Cobden*

Masters Degree, since the age difference between the two girls during their undergraduate years wasn't great enough to have made any substantive difference in the family's income.

Things may have been better by the time Marsh was doing her graduate work, but the family never had money for luxuries. Columnist John Downing was only one of many who commented on her childhood poverty when he wrote that "True could be tight with [the public]...dollar, due to her childhood in the genteel poverty of a Methodist manse."[24] In a short story she published in 1930 True conveyed very effectively the discomfort and general meanness of her "genteel poverty" in a passage describing the chair in which her minister protagonist sat. "The chair was not a comfortable one. Its back disdained the easy luxury of curves, and rose with puritan rigidity at a direct perpendicular just to the point where it could prod the spine with the maximum of discomfort. The seat was too shallow, the arms, too high and too wide apart for convenience, were not wide enough or sufficiently remote to be ignored. In a word, it was just such a chair as is always found in village parsonages, in cherry finish, to accompany a desk in golden oak."[25] Doris Tucker remembered True mentioning that she had had only one dress when she first went to Victoria College.

Perhaps the best description of True's almost hysterical rivalry towards her sister came through in a later interview when in describing how prayer helped calm her, she said, "I can remember as a child I was high strung and tense. I can remember dropping to my knees beside a mattress in a playroom...I couldn't have been more than seven and I asked God to please help me find my diary or my sister would get it. Not that she could have read it anyway."[26] [Marsh would have been only 5 years old at the time.]

It also shows something of the emotionalism of their lives. Isolated by their father's position and by frequent moves, True found making deep friendships difficult. The family was also intellectually and educationally separated from most of the parishioners in their country postings. Clara Thomas recalled that True and her friend, Edith Fowke "was born in Lumsden, Saskatchewan...and True's father was a minister there for awhile. When Edith was young she got to know True through the family because they had a lot of books and Edith was, from birth, a reader and during the Depression, of course, there were few books around and the Davidsons let her just walk in and out of their house and borrow their books at will."[27] True also described their library and that "Nobody tried to hold me from anything in my father's library. I read all of Shakespeare before I was nine. It was in a great big India paper edition, illustrated and unexpurgated."[28] Their isolation drove the family to seek everything from each other, intensifying all of their relationships.

True's early emotional loneliness formed a pattern which

continued for the rest of her life. Many who knew her commented on how, although a very social person, True had few close friends and that they felt she was a lonely woman. Doris Tucker remembered a "chap on the school board [who] said 'You're her friend for so long, then all of a sudden she gives you the boot...You'll find that she has a friend for awhile and then she'll drop him.' Myself, I used to say 'that's her Achilles heel. As soon as people get too close to her she pushes them away. You see. There's something about her background. She just doesn't trust people.'" Her nephew, David Cobden, remembered that she didn't really warm up to him until almost the end of her life although his wife said that, by then, True was extremely fond of him.[29] Charlotte Maher said that "when the purpose [for which she needed someone] ceased to be served she dropped them...the closest she was to anyone was to Emily Smith" but Emily said that True seldom shared her personal feelings or background with her.[30] Charlotte qualified her comment, however, by noting that "I really didn't care very much because it was all so exciting." [Being with True and meeting people True knew.]

Marsh was every bit as academically brilliant as True. Like her sister, she earned an M.A. from Victoria College, in her case, in Psychology. She worked at an Ontario mental health clinic, then travelled to Europe to study for a post-graduate degree with Dr. Alfred Adler in Vienna and at the University of London where she published two articles in the *British Journal of Medical Psychology*.[31] She was a member of the founding staff at Summerhill, the famous British alternative school. Marsh married in the late 1930s, moved to South Africa and had two sons.

She returned to Canada, with the two boys, in 1946 and stayed with True in Streetsville for a year. This was soon after their mother's death and may have been an attempt by Marsh to provide True with some of the support that she needed then.[32] While her children were still young and at boarding school, Marsh was diagnosed with terminal cancer. Her decision to leave her husband and children and come home to Canada to die may be the best possible illustration of the depth of attachment between the sisters, despite True's underlying rivalry. Marsh died soon after her arrival in Canada and was buried beside her parents. Her decision to return to Canada at that time was something her children never understood other than to say that "they [the Davidsons] were an unusual family."[33]

CHILDHOOD AND SCHOOL DAYS

True told few stories of her early years and even fewer of the people she had met then. Most of her childhood stories related to the places where she had lived and demonstrated her strong, poetic attachment to Canada's geography and history and her love of nature. She told one reporter that she had been born in a village near Montreal "on the shores of that Lake of Two Mountains that knew the steps of Champlain."[34]She recalled her father taking her to hear Sir Wilfrid Laurier talk when she was nine years old:

> I might as well say it, I was a precocious child, and when my younger sister was sleeping in my father's lap, there I was listening to that courtly, white-haired, dignified man—and thinking even then that what I wanted to be was a...politician.[35]

A common comment by those who knew True is that she rarely discussed her past, her family or other people. Her activities were constantly focussed on what she was doing now and her conversations were almost always about ideas. Several noted that she seemed to prefer talking to men, perhaps because she felt that their discussions were more likely to be of this sort. It was fascinating to note in Doris Pennington's book about Agnes MacPhail that Agnes had the same preferences.

> In a CBC tape [Agnes MacPhail's sister] said that at parties it was the custom for women to visit in one room, men in another, while the young people gathered in a third. Agnes was generally to be found with the men, "discussing such things as farm prices." Lilly would go after her and say, "Why don't you come in with the rest of us? We're playing cards." But Agnes would generally stay with the men.[36]

True's deepest attachments from her teenaged years were to the open lands of the prairies. One of her poems, quoted in part below, expressed her love of their natural beauty and the sense of emotional refreshment they gave her.

Land of Greatness

> I used to walk on the prairies,
> In the tangled, wild-flower spring

With the wet wind sweet on my forehead
And the migrant birds a-wing.
And life was a wonderful thing.

....

I must go back to the prairies,
For, whatever change I meet,
I must sense again the vastness
Of those miles of cattle and wheat,
Where earth and heaven meet.[37]

True began writing poetry at an early age and later claimed that the idea for her best poem was conceived when she was fifteen years old.[38] She excelled at school, matriculating from South Vancouver High School in 1915, then graduating from Regina Collegiate Institute.[39] One of her early resumes included information about her first summer job—working in a shoe store and doing playground work—followed by three summers of clerical work during 1917-19 for the Government of Saskatchewn, one year in the Treasury Department and two in the Education Department. Her final summer, between receiving her B.A. and entering Normal School (teacher's college), she worked for the Regina Public Library.[40]

True's mother had been instrumental in the formation of a C.G.I.T. group in Lumsden, Saskatchewan and True became one of its most active leaders. Sixty years later she recalled the day that she made her pledge as a Canadian Girl in Training in Saskatchewan.

> At the end of a conference we sang an old-fashioned song, "Beulah Land." I said, "For three days we have been living on the mountains, underneath a cloudless sky. Now we are parting and going down into the valleys. There will be clouds and sometimes we shall feel alone. But we shall not be alone and we shall remember the sun is still there even when we cannot see it. And we shall keep our pledge."[41]

Although its influence has decreased greatly in recent years, the C.G.I.T. provided leadership for many young women. According to *The Canadian Encyclopedia*, it "was established in 1915 by the Y.W.C.A. and the major Protestant denominations to promote the

Christian education of girls aged 12 to 17. Based on the small group whose members planned activities under the leadership of adult women, the program reflected the influence on Canadian Protestantism of progressive education, historical criticism of the Bible, the social gospel and Canadian nationalism."[42] The pledge, or purpose, that is still said aloud at meetings by both members and leaders had a large influence on True and reads:

> As a Canadian Girl in Training
> Under the leadership of Jesus
> It is my purpose to
>   Cherish health,
>   Seek truth,
>   Know God
>   Serve others
> And thus, with His help,
> Become the girl God would have me be.[43]

UNIVERSITY DAYS

A little more can be discovered about True's university days. She later recalled that: "My father sent me to Victoria, which is the first line of the college song. An awful song. My father sent me to Victoria and resolved that I should be a man. And so I settled down in the quiet college town on the old Ontario strand. That was when Victoria was at Cobourg."[44] She began her studies at Victoria in 1917 when she was only sixteen years old. A classmate recalled many years later that "she was the youngest and smartest student in the freshman class."[45] Clara Thomas knew several women who graduated from Victoria College around the same time as True and said that they all seemed imbued with the same drive, dedication and strong sense of ethics, whatever field they later entered. They were a small, select group. Women composed only a handful of Victoria's graduates at that time. They were also the first generation of female graduates empowered by womens' acquisition of the right to vote.

Once again, True excelled academically and was involved intensely in all the activities that the university had to offer. Margaret Addison, the Dean of Women, wrote in her letter of reference in 1922 that: "Miss Davidson has unusual ability, did very well in her college course, especially in English, in which she is exceptionally gifted. She has much originality and initiative; she is energetic, interested in games and in dramatics, in which she took a prominent part while at College."[46] The College Registrar and Associate Professor of English, C. E. Augery, noted in her reference letter that: "I can confidently say that she is one of the best students I have ever had....She has exceptional ability in debating and as an essayist and writer of verse. She is thoughtful and courageous and well qualified to exert a strong influence in any school fortunate enough to secure her services."[47]

Brandon Collegiate Institute, Manitoba. True taught English here in 1923 to help raise the money needed to return to Victoria University to take her Masters Degree. *Courtesy David Cobden*

In addition to topping her classes academically, True was active in a myriad of committees including the 4th Year Executive and the Women's Undergraduate Association and was President of the Women's Literary Social Executive. The information below her photograph in the 1921 yearbook read:

J.G. ("True") Davidson
"Laughter, Love and Tears"
Weaknesses —Class, Dramatic, "Y", Presidency of Literature

Strong Points—consuming chocolate bars, composing rhythmical
nonsense
Glory—Debates, oration contests
Shame—Last month's essay unwritten
Extraordinary—Passion, vitality, energy, nerve
Ordinary—Her "bete noir"
Past—Ubiquitous, various, rainbow-hued
Present—Flaming, intense, moody, alive
Future—Inky black or rosy gold.[48]

This photograph shows True, aged 16, wearing her C.G.I.T. uniform in 1917. *Courtesy
David Cobden*

There were very few
men at university in her
first years there. As she
later said, "We came in
the fall of 1917 and the
war wasn't over until the
next year. In our third
year there was a flood of
returned men. The whole
college changed and it was
quite an experience. A
sort of traumatic experi-
ence."[49] It is this reminder
of her age during World
War I that eliminates the
persistent rumour that
True never married be-
cause the man she loved
had been killed in battle.
She was 13 when the war
began and only 17 when it
ended. It is highly unlikely that she would have formed such a life-
altering attachment at that young age. What is perhaps more interesting is the need so many people have felt to invent a romantic reason for her not marrying.

In many ways, True was Victorian in her attitudes. She was
too Victorian to discuss the details of any romances and somewhat surprised that anyone would have the bad taste to ask, but
occasionally, in a naughty mood, she would acknowledge that she
had her opportunities. Clara Thomas remembered her class "dis-

cussing Sarah Jeannette Duncan's *The Imperialist*. "To the ears of the young in 1975 the dialogue sounds pretty stilted and one young man remarked that he simply couldn't believe that young people ever talked as Duncan wrote them."

"Indeed we did," said True. "When I first went to Victoria, we weren't allowed to have dances. We had Conversats, and we marched around the Great Hall to music. Then the veterans began to come back after the war, and they used to walk us right out of the room and upstairs to dark classrooms. And soon, we were allowed to have dances in the Great Hall—better to have dances in the light than students upstairs in the dark!"[50]

Agnes MacPhail recalled a similar entertainment at her high school where, once a year, "the young people walked around the auditorium in couples. When the music ended, the boy escorted the girl back to her seat and chose another partner for the next "promenade." At the last promenade the partners enjoyed a dish of ice cream together."[51]

True later told an interviewer that she had her romances, but that they were pretty tame.

> I was pretty innocent and unsophisticated and I thought if I were attracted to a man I must want to marry him and when …I found out about what went on between young men and young women…I think it turned me against the whole thing. If I wanted a man to kiss me I thought I ought to want to marry him and when I came back to Toronto in the Roaring Twenties, when people were lying down in swathes on the floor in darkened rooms and drinking themselves into stupors, it seemed to me all so sort of messy. I guess I'm a romantic. Any man I could talk to I would talk to. The only time we exchanged passes was if we couldn't think of anything to talk about. The result was that the men I had little affairs with, I don't think would have been happy with me any more than I would have been happy with them. I would have driven them crazy. They had a narrow escape. I think they realized they were well out of it. This is a sad fact of life. Women want men who are stronger than themselves, men they can look up to. I wouldn't have wanted to marry if I couldn't have made the man's interests mine… I grew up thinking I would find a man who was so strong and great and wonderful that I would be glad to spend the rest of my life looking after him and my children. And I just never found any such person.[52]

True learned to turn such questions into a joke. Many years later she told a student who asked why she never married that "....in my twenties I realized that I talked too much for any man, and I certainly didn't plan to give up talking."[53] Emily Smith told me that "with the right person she would have had a very much happier time. She didn't have that support system. She talked to me a lot but it wasn't like having a family."

Although True never found the person to whom she could give the complete dedication she felt essential for marriage, the thought that such a person might come along did not die right after university. Among her clippings from the early 1930s was one headed "Why I Asked Her to Marry Me. Ten Men Give Their Reasons."[54]

In 1922 True graduated from the Regina Normal School with her teaching certificate and immediately began work as a teacher/principal in Strasbourg, Saskatchewan. There she "taught English, History, Science and Art in all collegiate grades and was principal of a 3-room High School and a 5-room Public School."[55] What a killing task! She also won a magazine prize for the "Best CANADA Poem."[56]

The following year she moved to Brandon, Manitoba where she taught English at Brandon Collegiate, earning the money she needed to return to Victoria College to take her M.A. Once again, she excelled academically. Upon graduation she was offered a $350 scholarship from Bryn Mawr College in Pennsylvania to do post-graduate work there. She evidently declined on financial grounds, because they then wrote back with the offer of another half-scholarship,[57] but she was still unable to accept the offer.

It must have been a considerable disappointment to her to have to decline such an honour. Doris Tucker wondered whether it was a matter of finances, noting that "Bryn Mawr was a pretty toney place. She probably couldn't afford the clothes." Emily Smith felt that True wouldn't have liked going to teach in the United States because she was so attached to Canada. Clara Thomas suspects that True recognized the impossibility of a successful academic career for a woman in those days and knew that she should a better chance in business. It also may have been a matter of family obligations. Her father's eyesight began to fail him in 1925 and he returned to Ontario.[58] A later successful operation for cataract, then a very difficult medical procedure, restored his sight and he returned to work for a couple of years in 1938, but until then her parents were living in Toronto and needed her help. True returned to teaching, obtaining a post at Havergal Ladies' Academy where she taught History until 1926. That year, she began her next career, joining the staff at J.M. Dent and Sons Limited, Publishers, as the first female publishing sales representative in Canada.

2

THE DENT YEARS

1926–1930

"Twenty Years a Warrior,
Twenty Years a Chief, and
Twenty Years an Elder of the Tribe"

Clara Thomas recalled hearing True use the above quotation in conversation with a young woman who was sitting next to her on a flight back to Toronto from Ottawa. With minor variations in wording, it became True's favourite way of describing her lifetime of experiences.

True's decision not to accept the scholarships from Bryn Mawr marked the beginning of her years as a warrior. They were to prove to be years of triumph, hard times, disappointment, inspiration and personal loss.

Although she taught at several periods in her career, had definite opinions about teaching and derived considerable satisfaction from inspiring her students, True never regarded herself as a teacher. Teaching was only a marketable skill that she used when unable to earn a living as a writer.[1] Clara Thomas never heard her talk about teaching and noted that "I don't even know how long she taught…" She continued, however, that she knew "she had been at Dents for awhile." Doris Tucker similarly remembered little conversation about teaching, but did remember that "She always talked about Dents. She'd talk about her years there so I always felt that that was...a very important part of her working life." True, herself, later noted that "although my interests did not at first lie in that direction, I have spent most of my life in business,"[2] Hired in the summer of 1926 to sell books in the Toronto showroom and to screen all submitted manuscripts and decide which ones should be further reviewed by the firm's Managing Director, Mr. Henry Button, True rapidly undertook many other responsibilities. By the time she left the company in 1930 she was "responsible for all display advertising, catalogues and circulars, special exhibits, entertainments and stunt publicity...supervision of manufacturing in Canada and much of the correspondence with our London headquarters regarding Canadian manufacturing... check[ing] copyrights, look[ing] up illustrations...considerable editorial work...read[ing] proof of authorized texts and other important books...bookkeeping...supervis[ing] our...record of stock in London, our two Vancouver depositories and our two Toronto depositories, solv[ing] stock and sales discrepancies which hinder the preparation of royalty reports, ...prepa[ring] the annual budget and annual report...act[ing] as office manager, selecting and training new staff, representing the Managing Director on occasion and, most importantly, selling...on the road, working up educational authorizations, from Charlottetown to Victoria."[3]

A later interviewer wrote that "in those days, it was possible to publish books at a reasonable cost and have them authorized for certain grades for a certain number of years" and quoted True as saying,

> This was big business and I was the first woman to be in it. It involved spending four to eight weeks in a province at a time and becoming acquainted with ministers of education, deputy ministers, and superintendents and principals of normal schools [Teacher Colleges], and people with the power to advise the department of education, the textbook committees. This sort of thing. It was a big job. I was terrified. I was not really a saleswoman. I had lots of confidence in my...teaching, but I had never done anything like this before. At first I used to go back to my hotel room after each visit and try to work my courage up before I'd go out to the next one.[4]

Terrified she may have been but she didn't let it stop her. A copy of a
letter sent to Mr. Button in 1927 by D. McIntyre, the Superintendent of Winnipeg Schools and Chairman of the Advisory Board of
the Province of Manitoba, praised her selling abilities.

> I congratulate you on having so capable and tactful a representative
> as Miss Davidson. She made a very excellent impression on the peo-
> ple she met here. She pointed out to me most tactfully that the ap-
> pearance of the name of your house on the book lists was not as fre-
> quent as the merit of your books would justify, a position that I felt
> could not well be denied. [5]

Drawing of the Dent office, Aldine House, in Toronto. *Courtesy Reeta Wright*

J.M. Dent and Sons was a British company, headquartered in
London, dealing mainly in classics, encyclopedias, and school
texts. The Canadian Branch Office was located in a converted
house on Bloor Street in Toronto. True's secretary from those
days, Reeta Wright, remembers it as "a beautiful building...with a
beautiful library... and a lovely overgrown back garden with a
trellised path surrounded by rose bushes...[it was] the only place I
ever worked, right out of Business College, [I] felt very lucky that I
had such a lovely place to work." The house stood somewhat
alone "there wasn't much along Bloor there" on the north side of

Interior view of the showroom and office of Aldine House. True and her secretary worked in the alcove part-way up the steps leading from the showroom.
Courtesy Reeta Wright

Bloor Street, "just across the road from McMaster University [now the Royal Conservatory of Music] and the stadium was just at the corner." The office had a small staff. Mrs. Wright remembers only "the Managing Director and his Secretary, True and me, the caretaker and that's about all." She also remembers it as a generally friendly, but not chummy, office. "Mr. Button called her [True] Davey all the time...he called me Tiny Tim...they treated me like family...indeed Mr. Button wrote me a letter advising me when I was getting married...telling me the problems I might face...I said he was talking to me like a father would and he said 'I feel like that about you." She said that True didn't talk about her personal life at all, but neither did she, "it didn't seem appropriate at the office." She mainly remembered True being "wrapped up in her business world and her book sales...True and I got along alright. She'd tell me what she wanted and I'd just go and do it....I did as I was told. I guess I was kind of young and green then too...she was just herself and I was just myself...she was just my boss and I got along with her...those were happy years with True." They didn't take lunch together. Reeta often ate hers alone in the back garden and she couldn't "ever recall True eating even." She did remember True sending her a letter during one of her selling trips out West in which True had said "I bragged about you like a hen with one chick." She couldn't recall any of True's family visiting her at work and certainly no male friends. They did a lot of correspondence with MacMillan's and other publishers and there were constant reports to be typed to the London office.

They worked the standard office hours of the time, 9-5, six days a week. Mrs. Wright remembered True's hours as being "pretty regular. She was there when I got in in the morning. We didn't waste too much time. We'd get right down to work and of course I was taking dictation and then I'd be typing it out and she'd be on the phone. She was on the phone a lot of the time...talking to other publishers...I didn't pay any attention to what she was saying, I was too busy."

Mrs. Wright and her husband remembered True as being "fairly mannish in her ways, and sharp with her tongue, but she never lambasted anybody—she would just catch you up if she thought you were wrong." She was "so kind of plain...anything but beautiful," dressed in "suits, plain, mannish. To me she always looked the same... slim and tall [with] short hair, just like a brush cut." If True got upset "she really didn't spare her language. If she felt like swearing, she'd swear. Unusual then, but she was slightly mannish in some of her ways...but she was a born developer and promoter, so yes, so she wasn't shy in her mannerisms, but we got along great."[6]

I suspect that True felt it desirable to seem "mannish" while serving as Canada's first female publishers representative, just as at other times in her career, she would use her feminity where it seemed appropriate or useful. Also, she was still trying to assess herself and her future. Among the clippings in her files are several from this time period with headings like, "How to Get On with the Crowd," "Break the Ice of Loneliness," "Your Emotions Can Make You Sick," and "Twelve Things to Avoid if You Want to Be a Success."[7]

Certainly she impressed her male colleagues. Among her papers was a little card from the President of the MacMillan Company of Canada in which "HSE" has written:

We have a young lady in view,
To whom an apology's due,
We admit—thought with pain
That we rifled the brain
That is almost too good to be True.[8]

This rare casual photograph of a relaxed and laughing True (in centre) was taken in the overgrown rose trellis area behind the J.M. Dent offices at Aldine House. Also shown is her secretary, Reeta Wright (front). The third woman was the secretary to the firm's Managing Director, Mr. Henry Button. *Courtesy Reeta Wright*

In those years True had to learn many hard lessons about the business world; lessons she didn't feel she had been taught at home or at school. In 1930 she condensed some of these lessons into a paragraph in a book review published in *The Business Woman*.

'My face is my fortune, sir,' she said, and it was all very well for the little girl in the nursery rhyme to say so; but most of us are less fortunate. We must carve out the fortunes for ourselves, if fortunes there are to be; and many of us have about as much idea of how to

go at the matter as we would have of how to attack an actual block
of marble with hammer and chisel. Men seem to have some sort of
instinct in these things—I am sure no lad ever approached an employment officer in a bank with the statement that he would love to
work in a bank because he was so fond of money...Yet scores
of...girls...have come to me during the years of my connection with
the Dent Publishing Company, pleading for a place on our staff because they were so fond of books...[9]

True may not have started out wanting to work in publishing,
but she came to believe that she was doing worthwhile work, especially when it encouraged the development of Canadian literature.
During a talk she gave in 1928 she said, "that Canadian publishers
were fostering Canadian literature at a financial sacrifice...[and
that] anyone who did anything to promote Canadian literature was
doing a service to his country...Canadian literature could do a lot
for the Dominion. It would help to unify the vast areas that are
now more or less separated...Everyone could not travel and the
next best method of familiarizing oneself with conditions and people in other parts of a vast country was to read about them."[10]
True already had a skillful speaking presence; the newspaper report
of her talk noted that she "spoke in a humorous vein."

One of the more demanding parts of her job seems to have
been the rejection of manuscripts. Some were easier to reject than
others. She told the Kiwanians that "it was unnecessary to read a
whole manuscript in order to determine whether it was publish-
able or not. Very often one page was enough to settle that point.
Sometimes, she said, she saved up half a dozen offerings and dealt
with them over the weekend." She also found that many would-be
authors had unrealistic expectations of possible financial returns,
telling them "of a young girl who brought in a novel and without
waiting to ascertain whether or not it would be published demanded a 50-50 split with the firm. That meant, if the book re-
tailed for two dollars that the authoress would get a dollar while
the publishers would have to give a discount to the bookseller, pay
the expenses of writing and marketing and accept what was left as
profit." The book wasn't accepted so "there was no need to haggle
over financial details."[11]

Other times it was harder. Reeta Wright remembered that
"she hated to disappoint them, especially the younger people that

This photograph was taken around 1930 when True travelled to England where she represented the Canadian Managing Director, Henry Button, at the English head office of J.M. Dent and Sons. Her secretary, Reeta Wright, remembered her as looking "very mannish" with her short hair. *Courtesy David Cobden*

would expect some reaction she couldn't give." One of True's short stories, written around this time, included a character, Maridell, the daughter of a minister, who had to assess a book submitted by a minister who reminds her very much of her father.

...Maridell left the "Pilgrims of Peace" as long as she dared. Finally, one day, "I daren't read this manuscript," she said to her chief, "I wish you'd take a look at it."

He glanced through a few pages. What Maridell brought him was usually well worth serious consideration. Thus it took him a few minutes

to realize the nature of the work. Then he threw it down, amazed, infuriated. "Putrid!" he roared. "Hopeless! What do you mean by asking me to read such tripe? Shoot it back." Then as she hesitated,
"What's the matter? Don't stand there looking like a sick cat!"
"I felt sorry for him," she murmured lamely. "He was a minister—
from the country."
Her employer exploded, "If we were to weep over every fool that
thought he could write, the world would be flooded...Pah! Take it
away. It makes me sick just to look at it."
What could Maridell do? Sometimes one grew very weary of working
in a publishing house, but she supposed there were unpleasant features
about any job. She shrugged her shoulders and dictated a letter.[12]

During her years at Dents, True worked on several books and
is sometimes credited as the author [more accurately the editor] of
a childrens' book, *Canada in Story and Song*. She also wrote poetry and short stories, several of which were later published.

While working at Dents that she had her first real contact with
the left-wing intellectuals who later inspired her to join the Co-op-
erative Commonwealth Federation (C.C.F.). J.M. Dent & Sons
published the *Canadian Forum* during her years there so she had
the opportunity to meet several of its contributors, including historian Frank Underhill and law professor Frank R. Scott who later
formed the League for Social Reconstruction. The League was a
major influence on the founding of the C.C.F. and played a large
role in the writing of its declaration of principles, "The Regina
Manifesto." The philosophy of their magazine, described as
"avowedly nationalist and progressive, and usually on the left of
the spectrum on political and cultural issues"[13] was familiar to
True since it mirrored the "social gospel" ideals popular in the
Methodist church of her childhood and which formed much of the
philosophy behind the C.G.I.T. which had influenced her teenage
years. The social gospel "sought to apply Christianity to the col-
lective ills of an industrializing society...and held an optimistic
view of human nature and entertained high prospects for social reform. By W.W. I it had become a principal informing principle of
social reform."[14]. The movement had particularly strong support
in western Canada, where it was led by charasmatic leaders like
James Shaver Woodsworth.
In 1930, True reached the pinnacle of her publishing career

when she was sent to England, on behalf of the Canadian office, "to negotiate financial arrangements and expedite the preparation of various text books."[15] She resigned her position with the company almost immediately afterwards, leading to speculation as to what happened during that business trip to London that caused her to leave what had been, thus far, an exceptionally successful career.

Clara Thomas felt that True was "always very restless...things never really did satisfy her. She was always going on, looking ahead." It does seem that True was never satisfied with any position for very long and certainly not with one where she couldn't reach the top. But her decision was prompted by more than restlessness. In her 1930 resume she listed as her "Reasons for Wishing to Leave—[the] Impossibility of specialization in so small a firm, and thus impossibility of any further development whatsoever, except that of succeeding Mr. Button, remote by 20 years, and unlikely even then in view of my sex and the conservative feeling of our London principals."[16] This final phrase provides some idea of what was likely said to her at the London head office. Dents would not have been unique in their resistance to the idea of a woman advancing to become a managing director. After all, the Supreme Court (then still in Britain) had only recently ruled that "women were persons under the law" and thus eligible for appointment to the Canadian Senate.

However discouraged True may have become about her chances in the publishing field, she remained confident enough to state clearly what were then considered decidedly feminist demands. Describing the "Type of Position Desired" she wrote "something which will use all my energy...in which having the strength, perseverance and courage of a man, I shall be permitted to go as far as a man of parallel ability."[17]

3

A STRUGGLING WRITER

1930–1931

*T*rue couldn't have chosen a worse time to leave a secure position; just as the Canadian economy slid into the decade-long "Great Depression". All began well. She was hired almost immediately by the Canadian Federation of University Women as the Managing Director of their Vocational Bureau to "help university girls find their niche in business life."[1] The Bureau supported itself from the fees that it collected for filling a position, but, at a time when thousands of experienced men were unable to find work, the Bureau soon found it impossible to earn enough fees to continue and was closed in July 1931.

Her reference letter from the Convenor of the Vocational Committee responsible for the Bureau noted that True had "carried on the work in a splendid manner. She has the qualities of insight, understanding, and objectiveness necessary for vocational guidance, as well as those of initiative and executive ability which must be part of a successful director."[2] A less formal letter sent to True by all of the members of the Vocational Committee, thanked her for her work and noted that "With very little renumeration, and no immediate prospect of any, you have cheerfully and successfully carried on through a time of unprecedented business and economic depression. We feel that this has been a particularly fine and unselfish achievement."[3] I suspect from this that in her work at the Bureau, True had found, at least briefly, the calling she constantly sought. Many years later she quoted Dr. Robert McClure as saying that you don't need money, "but you do need to be useful."[4]

The pain of losing her position at the Vocational Bureau was moderated by the thrill of winning the first prize in the annual contest of Canadian writers of the Women's Canadian Club. In April 1931 she was awarded its $100 prize in a ceremony in the concert hall of the King Edward Hotel. This was a major award. It was only the second time in eleven years that the Club had offered its prize for poetry and True defeated 190 other contestants from as far away as Siam to win. Stories about her win appeared in all of the major Toronto papers.

The poem, "Muses of the Modern Day" was, she said, "designed to meet the contention of many that modern subject matter did not lend itself to poetry."[5] According to a newspaper account she said "with much modesty" that winning the prize "had given her the most thrilling moment of her life." The same article also noted that "she had written poetry since she was five years old, but it was not until a little over a year ago that she submitted any for publication" and quoted her as saying "It was not until after I left the publishing company that I had courage to submit my poetry for publication. I had been subdued by the horror of being one of those awful persons whose perpetrations editors dread."[6] True continued to regard herself as being first and foremost a writer for the rest of her life. Charlotte Maher told me that True always "saw herself as a researcher and writer. What she was, was one terrific politician, but that wasn't part of her image of herself." Doris Tucker remembered a time when all the municipal candidates had to list their occupation. True first wrote down "Mayor" but, when Doris told her she couldn't do that, changed it to writer. In a column written after her retirement from politics, True talked about how after leaving public life she had moved "into the field of study and writing, where I [have] always felt I really belonged."[7]

Encouraged by the win, True succeeded in having several poems published that year. She wrote a number for articles for various publications, including *The Canadian Forum, The New Outlook,* and *The Globe and Mail.* Her first magazine story, "Help Wanted," was published in the September 1931 issue of *Chatelaine.* It is difficult to determine how many of her poems, stories and plays were published since only a few of her manuscripts have also been kept in printed form among her papers. She also submitted manuscripts under many pseudonyms in-

cluding the names Susan Finnie, Margaret Danelaw, Bard Pente-
cost, E.S.B. Finnie, Peggy Dane, Maple Wilder, and, believe it or
not, Flower LeStrange!

J.M. Dent & Sons published a book of her poetry, called
Muses of the Modern Day and Other Days, that same year which
received excellent reviews. A.M. Stephen wrote in *The Vancouver
Province* that:

> Miss Davidson...will challenge comparison with any of the women
> who are given prominence among Canadian poets....Her best lines
> and many of her poems ring with sincerity and carry
> conviction....Strength is seldom an outstanding characteristic of the
> artistic work of women. Yet, if we are to have poetry expressive of
> this modern age, it will have to be more than decorative or reminis-
> cent of the modes of a bygone day....She is alive to the fact that this
> is the age of machinery, of psychology, of intellectual unrest and dis-
> illusion. This author can think. Her work is valuable because it mir-
> rors the reactions of a sensitive woman who has faced life shoulder
> to shoulder with men and who has bravely taken the bitter with the
> sweet in the struggle for existence. Her poetry reflects life rather than
> the "the realms of gold" in which the sheltered woman takes refuge
> from reality.[8]

E.J. Pratt's review in *The Canadian Student* noted that "this little
book of poems...is marked by a distinct individuality and by a light
lyrical movement which never gives the impression of mere facility
...there is no trace of immaturity in the work. The forms are varied
but always under fine control and—what is just as gratifying—the
content is rich enough to repay reflection on the part of the reader.
One realizes that the writer has something to say as well as to feel,
that underneath the moods there is a basis of ideas."[9]

Although a critical success, the book enjoyed only limited
commercial success. Perhaps that is why True clipped and kept
among her papers a poem by Frances Bragan Richman which
began, " They tell me poetry doesn't pay/And they're right, I suppose, in a practical way. Since what does it profit a rose to
bloom/Like a lamp in summer's living room?"[10]

With the loss of her salary from the Vocational Bureau, True
had to scramble to supplement the small income made from her
writing. Her letterhead from 1932 listed her as doing "Manuscript

Criticism, Revision, Research, Statistical Work, Typing, Placement"[11] and there is a small advertising card in her files in which she advertised a course for "Current Literature Groups" that she was leading. The same flyer also advertised that she would provide special lectures on topics as varied as, "The Straw Scarecrow and other Dictators, The Matriarchal Tradition, These Crazy Poets, A Trip to China in Novel

True Davidson, 1923, age 22. *Courtesy David Cobden*

Company, Women at War" and noted that she would provide "similar Topical Talks for professional and other specialized organizations. Fees according to numbers and purpose."[12] Among some of the groups to whom she spoke were the Lyceum Women's Art Association, where she criticized modern poetry, and the Lynbrook School Dramatic Club, where she spoke about amateur theatricals, "stressing the possibilities and pitfalls open to beginners."[13] Many years later, True was asked by a shy student about her public speaking. Clara Thomas wrote that "the reply was one of the most unforgettable pictures of True that she treated us to. "I practise in front of a mirror," she said. "I've practised all over, sometimes in hotel rooms, before a mirror, wearing the hat I'm going to speak in, and my slip."[14]

Another of her schemes was an attempt to work up orders for a book of poems from the shop owners along Bloor Street which they could use both as advertising and as incentives for their customers. Under this enterprising scheme she proposed to publish 1,000 copies of her poems which had been inspired by the scenes along Bloor Street; to sell three hundred of them through bookstores; and to distribute the remaining seven hundred to a selected list of addresses in Rosedale and the Annex or (for an extra fee) to the preferred customers of the sponsoring firms along with their card. All advertisers were to have their name and address also shown at the bottom of the poem they had inspired.[15] She got an estimate on the cost of printing the book from the T.H. Best Printing Co. which described it as having "64 pages...28 pages small cuts, quarter bound, cloth back and paper board sides." She went as far as to have them prepare dummies in October 1933[16], but she was never able to sign up sufficient subscribers to have it published.

While her money-making activities were a constant struggle, True enjoyed several successes in other areas as she continued her involvement with left-wing organizations and took part in debates and other activities at the university and with the University Women's Club and the Business and Professional Women's Club. A review of one of this latter group's debates noted that "the subject of the debate was: "Resolved, that business women make the best wives." The affirmative was upheld by Miss Jane McDowall and Miss Helen Lynn, and Miss True Davidson and Miss Mary Dale Muir were on the negative side. The argument proved an amusing one, and the result was lost in the laughter of the audience."[17] At another debate, the University of Toronto Womens' Union declared that they would prefer to be Agnes MacPhail than film star Mary Pickford.[18]

Her involvement in left-wing organizations likely began from her contacts with the League for Social Reconstruction and the *Canadian Forum* and was strengthened by her own financial struggles and by the conditions observed while she worked at the Vocational Bureau.

In April 1931, True was awarded a $100 prize from the Women's Canadian Club for "the best poem written in Canada that year." Shortly afterwards a collection of her poetry was published which received several glowing reviews and which heralded her work as challenging in "comparison with any of the women who are given prominence among Canadian poets." *Courtesy David Cobden*

One of her earliest activities helped the Toronto Branch of the Women's International League for Peace and Freedom set up a book-room.[19] The wife of one of True's professors, Anna N. Sissons, was the corresponding secretary for this organization and it was at her home that True had lunch with J.S. Woodsworth and experienced what she later described as an "old-fashioned religious conversion." This led her join the C.C.F. in 1934, only two years after it was founded.[20] Professor C.B. Sissons, a University of Toronto classicist, was Woodsworth's cousin and had been the best man at his wedding. In a later interview she repeated that she "was first attracted to socialism by J.S. Woodsworth, the C.C.F. leader...[because of his]...love for people. You could warm your hands in his personality."[21] Woodsworth was about the same age as her father and his dedication, deep sense of calling and ministerial experiences in the western provinces doubtless reminded her strongly of him. Although Woodsworth had considerable influence on politics and on the provision of social services in Canada, he was far from a typical politician. He was driven by ideals rather than the necessities of maintaining political power, although he negotiated many very successful compromises. Once again True had found a sense of calling. As Walter Young wrote in his book, *The Anatomy of a party: The National C.C.F. 1932-1961* "... the socialism of the CCF inspired service and sacrifice; it was a faith [its members felt] worth crusading for since it offered everything that was good and opposed all that was bad.[22] Woodsworth told a national convention, "In our efforts to win elections we must not yield to the temptations of expediency. Let us stick to our principles, win or lose."[23] Although, like the majority of the party, True later supported the declaration of war against Germany in 1939, it was Woodworth's principled stand against it that she remembered best and later included in a short poem.

Opponents said to J.S. Woodsworth once
(The noted pacifist), "We must fight fire
With fire," but, smiling gently, he replied
"Fight fire with water, rage with peace, and hate
With patient understanding and with strong
Persistent loving and with tireless faith....[24]

Throughout her life True collected odd newspaper clippings and wrote out quotations which appealed to her. Among these are some which reveal aspects of her thoughts and feelings about the party. One of these quotes, attributed by her to Grover Cleveland's "Annual Message for 1888", said "The Communism of combined wealth and capital...[is]...not less dangerous than the communism of oppressed poverty and toil." Another noted that "Socialism inevitable if world wants to avoid Communism" and another, somewhat sadly, that "Those of us who are in earnest must be ready to face antagonism, ostracism."[100]

Her experiences in the Depression showed in one of her poems entitled, "Free Enterprise."

> "My little plant," the manufacturer said
> With modest praise, leading his guest by row,
> On row of trembling girls, who worked below
> The earth-line, in his cellars. Pale as snow
> The flowers in their cheeks. That was a bed
> Where only livid parasites could grow.
>
> He did not feel the cold. Rotund, well-fed,
> He did not know his plant's deep roots were dead.[101]

True's friend, Emily Smith, suspected that True liked the C.C.F. because "the odd parties had an appeal for her...they were not strong the way old political parties were...they didn't have the cohesiveness...she would have liked stepping in and getting it going...but if you get into a party thats already established [you can't do that] ..." While True's support for the C.C.F. slowly waned over the years as many of the social welfare issues she supported were implemented by the other parties and as she became increasingly uncomfortable with the growing importance of labour unions within the party, she remained an active supporter until shortly before the C.C.F. joined with the Canadian Labour Congress to form the New Democratic Party.

4

WORKING FOR PERKINS BULL

1931–1938

*I*n late 1931, True was hired by William Perkins Bull to collect a library of Canadiana which he wished to give as a wedding present to his son whose home was going to be in England. About 400 first editions were desired, together with the autographs of the authors, of the illustrators, of the editors and of the subjects of biographies.[1] True's work on this project must have impressed Bull because he then appointed her his Chief of Staff, in charge of all the personnel, male and female, engaged in researching and producing his histories of Peel County. Bull's original intention had been to produce one 50-60 page book on the subject, but the project soon grew into an obsession. He hired scores of researchers and interviewers and began production of a remarkable series of books that Augustus Bridle of *The Toronto Daily Star* described as "a delightful hodgepodge of history and biography written with the guile of an ancient mariner." Topics ranged from the history of sports to military undertakings to the Orange Order to the life of Sitting Bull. He hired some of the best artists in the country to illustrate them.[2] True was quoted as assuring the reporter that "if it sounds as though we were going far afield, let me assure you that is only because of ramifications made by early Peel settlers and their affairs."[3] In another article she was quoted as asserting that she "considers Mr. Bull's undertaking the most important piece of historical research ever undertaken in Canada, and…only a wealthy and extremely public-spirited man could do it."[4]

It was certainly a big project. The same article stated that "Miss Davidson is in charge of practically all details of the work.

True began working for William Perkins Bull in 1931 and rose to be second-in-command of his extensive staff of researchers, writers and illustrators. True later said of him that he was "a robber baron in the wrong age...but I grew very fond of him." *Courtesy the Metropolitan Toronto Reference Library*

Her staff consists normally of 20 but has run up to 70. A tremendous amount of research work has to be done: looking thro [sic] private files, letters, newspapers, libraries and by personal interview. Everything is traced to prove its authenticity."[5] The books were produced in limited quantities and most were given to libraries and museums. In 1938, True told a Regina reporter that "three out of the 20 central staff members are working on old family histories of Peel people. These sketches occupy 32 large steel files and include the complete record of every 25 acres in Peel from the original crown grant. Four of the staff members are stenographers; two are filing clerks, and three are artists. Indexing, proof reading, summarizing newspaper articles of ancient date, all this is part of the undertaking."[6] Several sources have cast doubt on how much of the writing of these books was actually done by Bull, or whether he acted more as an editor, using the very comprehensive writings of his research staff and of True Davidson. None of the books credits anyone other than Bull by name, a decision for which many criticized him later. True, however, knew that her work would not be acknowledged by anything other than a paycheque. As an article written at the time noted "...while Miss Davidson's name will not appear in these works, and will be forgotten when the books are remembered and prized, there is no doubt but that her work, in them, will remain."[7] The same article noted that "Miss Davidson is largely responsible for the compilation of the material, and naturally, while Mr. Bull himself is the authority, he must depend on someone who has a background of historical research, knows something of apt illustration, of binding, and all the other details which follow the gathering of the material itself."[8] True was realist enough to recognize that the employment opportunities for writers, researchers and illustrators during the Depression were too few for any of them to be able to insist upon written acknowledgment as well.

The paycheque had to suffice, but there is also some doubt about how regularly it arrived. Doris Tucker remembers True telling her about a time when she had to march into a large dinner party that Bull was having and demand that he pay "the girls" so they could go home for Christmas. "She never said an awful lot about how he behaved, just about him not paying the girls and I just wondered if at the time whether she got paid." Harry Evans, who came to know True while she lived in Streetsville, remembered his mother saying that "[True] hated Perkins Bull because he didn't pay her ..."[9] His older brother, Garfield Evans, wrote to me that:

> "I can remember one of the men talking about being questioned by this woman. Quite a discussion followed. It seems a lot of them had been questioned. ...[Many years later while staying with his brother] he handed me a book and I nearly fell over. "Peel's Fighting Men" by some big wheel that had a master farm and piles of money named "Bull." It was True Davidson that did all the work. She did the whole thing, interviews, pictures, before and after and it must have been a hell of a job. Now get this. He never paid her! The big stuffed shirt got away with it.[10]

However, in later interviews, True always spoke well of Perkins Bull. "He was a very shrewd man, a good businessman. He paid me a proper screw [a good salary] and this was during the Depression when people were working for nominal sums."[11] She was likely all the more grateful for being given a position of such responsibility at a time when there was considerable public pressure to force women to return to the home and leave the jobs for the unemployed men. True described Bull as "a robber baron in the wrong age...but I grew very fond of him."[12] I doubt that she would have been so generous in her comments if he had cheated her consistently. The book mentioned by Garfield Evans came out after True had left Bull's employ, while he was under newspaper attack and gossip prompted by the death of his guest, an American heiress, Mabelle Horlick Sidley. Mrs. Sidley had been a major financial contributor to Bull's historical projects. One newspaper interview of the time quoted Bull defending the money (estimated at $1-1.5 million) Mrs. Sidley had spent by saying that "it was spent among friends and in works in which she was enormously interested...She followed this work closely and took great delight in its progress....It was spent in harmony with the way in which her father and her mother and her brother...lavished their cash and gifts...on things in which they were interested and which appealed to them as being worthy."[13]

Perkins Bull is another name about which there have been rumours of a romantic attachment on True's part. Charlotte Maher told me that "... if you wanted to be romantic you might almost think there was something going on there [with Bull], you might almost have thought there was." Clara Thomas doubted this, however. "True wasn't that interested....I pity the man who made a real pass at her including Perkins Bull. He would have met his match." Certainly Bull respected her abilities. In a letter sent to a friend in Regina he called her "my right hand man" and asked that "Should it be convenient to give her a friendly handshake on my account, I will appreciate it. Such of the folk of Regina who happen to meet her will, I think, find her a young lady of parts and attainments."[14]

True doubtless enjoyed working with yet another strong, dominant man, one who had experienced an exciting life and who was devoting himself to a project which she highly valued. She said of him "Mind you, he was a tartar. But so was Fred Gardiner. You know, in a way W.P. and Fred Gardiner were quite a bit alike. Both of them were big heavy set men and both of them were pretty domineering. I'm pretty domineering myself and I used to fight with W.P. in his day just as I fought with Fred in the one year I was on Metro Council with him."[15] True always loved a good fight and had a grudging respect for those who fought her best. Bull was married, a devoted parent who wrote to his children weekly, and the same age as her father. If True felt any romantic attraction towards him, she was unlikely to have acknowledged it to herself—or to him. Additionally, whatever she may have felt for him, his style of life was very different from that which she had been raised to respect.

Descended from a prosperous pioneering family which had produced several clergymen and successful farmers, William Perkins Bull was born in 1870, the eldest son of Bartholomew Bull and Sarah Duncan Bull of Brampton. Lucy Booth Martyn says of them that they "owned the largest herd of Jersey cattle in the world—it was considered amusing for local residents to tell innocent outsiders that they got their milk from Bulls!"[16]

Bull was described as a "big man, with a distinctive curly beard at a time when beards were unusual.[17] Another article wrote that "by the 1930s, he had grown to look remarkably like the former king, Edward VII. He was over 6 feet tall, heavily built, magnificently bewhiskered and often wore a black cutaway suit with a black satin waistcoat. He was, to say the least, a commanding figure."[18] He had enjoyed an adventurous career, engaging in Arctic explorations, trips with surveying parties in the western provinces and with inspectors of Indian reserves.[19] It is stated that "from his earliest days as a student, Bull had vowed that one day he would be rich and famous and by the time he was 30 he was both. He had a brief and rather inauspicious career as a lawyer in Toronto. By 1910, through his unaccountable talent for making money and a somewhat flamboyant way of investing it, he had acquired a 25,000 acre plantation in Cuba and, shortly afterwards, launched a 50,000-acre development scheme in western Canada."[20] He also became founder and director of Ingram and Bell, founder and president of the Okanagan Lumber Company of British Columbia, founder, director and treasurer of Mississauga Lumber Company and president of Sterling Oil Company of Ohio.[21]

He owned three enormous homes: one in Cuba, another in Toronto at 3 Meredith Crescent in Rosedale and a third in London, England. During World War I he had financed and operated the Perkins Bull Hospital for Canadian soldiers in a large house across the street from his London home.[22] He was famous for the liberality of his hospitality, entertaining the families of the wounded officers in his home on several occasions, and was known in the highest circles of London society during the war years. The newspapers even claimed that he had been a personal friend of King George V.[23]

Bull did the majority of his writing in the dining room of his Toronto house, Lorne Hall, while True worked in its library, which he called the "Book Room." Martyn described the house as having "replicas of bulls... everywhere...The large mat outside the front door...had a bull pictured on it, while statuettes of bulls in china, glass and bronze stood on tables and mantels, and pictures of bulls hung on the walls....the platter in the dining room of Lorne Hall showed a magnificent bull. Even the blue end papers of the Peel County histories carried a large bull, as did William's stationery...These numerous bulls were all well-endowed and provided much conversation, frequently ribald."[24]

Bull had wanted fame as well as wealth and, if fame is measured in column-inches of newspaper copy, he achieved that goal too. During one of his many trips across the Atlantic to Britain, he met Colonel William Horlick, who had become a multimillionaire from the sales of his patented "Horlick's Malted Milk." Bull soon became a close friend of the Colonel's daughter, Mabelle Horlick Sidley, and acted as her lawyer when she sought a divorce from her husband, Dr. John Streeter Sidley. This case was long and nasty. At one point Dr. Sidley sued Mr. Bull and his wife, alleging injury to health through shadowing and harassment from detectives. Then, the federal narcotics squad raided Mr. Bull's and Mrs. Sidley's apartments on suspicion that they were dealing in drugs or some other illegal activity. Nothing was found and both were given a formal apology. The police in tapping their telephones had misinterpreted the codes and signals they were using in connection with her divorce action. Bull was quoted at the time as saying, "They are great wire tappers down there, I am not losing any sleep over the matter."[25] Mrs. Sidley eventually obtained her divorce. Her husband died five years later.

Then, Bull was involved in a traffic accident near Quincy, Michigan, and although considered in serious condition, insisted upon being taken to Canada for treatment. This led to yet more pages of newspaper speculation, including suggestions that he had been in flight from Al Capone and his gang, a story which Bull always denied.

Bull had a talent for getting newspaper coverage, even when not involved in court cases. While True Davidson was in Regina, researching a book about Sitting Bull for him, the newspapers reported that Bull had told an audience "that the United States was

founded by Communists and criminals." The same article quoted
True as admitting "that it was startling, but...Mr. Bull was known
for his disturbing way of backing such statements by historical
facts..."[26] The historical basis later given for this statement was
the fact that Britain had sent convicts to the United States before
the prison colonies were established in Australia and that the Puri-
tans were Communists because "they held property in common
and shared the proceeds of their labour" during their first years of
settlement.[27] True also was to become famous for her use of effective "quotable quotes" when dealing with the media. Did she
learn the art from Perkins Bull?

During her seven years with Bull, True continued to write and
submit short stories and articles for magazines. She joined and became an active member of the C.C.F., working mainly in the educational branch, writing and assisting with courses. Among the
material she wrote for them was an article, "Our Canadian Heritage," a play, "Out of This Nettle" on which she wrote the note,
"performed at various C.C.F. meetings throughout Toronto and
elsewhere. Could be altered by susbstitution of socialist or reform
for C.C.F."[28]

Her major outside activity, however, was with several small
theatre groups around Toronto. She wrote a number of plays, including "An Elizabethan Christmas" which she noted was "originally presented by the Credit Valley Drama League and Junior
Players", and "Independent Minds," which was produced by the
University College Players Guild, under the title *An Academic
Problem*. She was heavily involved with a new theatre group, The
Fountain Players. *The Toronto Star* reported that she directed one
play and then, in 1934, wrote and produced a new 3-act play
called "All the Rivers" which was a humorous "study of Canadian, English and United States' national types."[29] A review of
this play among her papers, from an unidentified newspaper, said
that the play made a "favorable impression...a distinct hit with
the audience...The outstanding triumph of the evening, however,
was Miss Davidson's. She displayed a very pretty wit and a rare
gift for writing deft and sparkling dialogue, which should carry
her far in the field of lighter Canadian drama."[30] *The Telegram*,
however, was less complimentary about another production in
which she was involved, mocking her comment that the costumes
were "home-made...all at a cost (according to Directress Miss

True Davidson) of under five dollars."[31] True maintained an interest in amateur and semi-professional dramatics throughout the rest of her life, both as a participant and as a regular subscriber.

True's final project for Perkins Bull involved her in doing research about the life of Sitting Bull which required her to travel to Saskatchewan in February 1938. She resigned shortly afterwards. Following a successful operation for his cataracts, her father had acquired a new charge in Kenilworth where she moved to live with her parents. It is likely that they needed her help. Her father was now past normal retirement age and her mother was an invalid. The suddeness of True's resignation leads to speculation that there may have been some dispute between her and Bull. However, there is nothing in her papers to confirm or deny this suspicion.

It is probable that True had also been responsible for lining up another publicity stunt for Perkins Bull during her trip west. A few months later, he told a reporter that "he had intended observing [his 68th birthday] in western Canada...[where] he was to have been made a chief of the Sioux Indian tribe in Saskatchewan. ...While in the west...he was to be given a complimentary dinner, and was scheduled to make an address in Saskatoon."[32]

Bull was unable to enjoy his unique birthday celebration because he was under subpoena for an inquest into the death of his friend, Mabelle Horlick Sidley, who had died in his home on July 6th. Her death provoked a virtual newspaper feeding frenzy. The Toronto newspapers suggested that Bull had influenced Mrs. Sidley to make a will in his favour when she was of unsound mind; told stories about the bars installed on her bedroom windows on Bull's orders; quoted Bull's chauffeur as saying that she gave cheques for very large sums to friends and associates and handed out cash to complete strangers. Rumours of possible foul play ran rampant. The story acquired all the elements necessary to remain on the front page news for months when it was revealed that Mrs. Sidley had left Bull $250,000 outright and a third of her residual estate, first estimated at $7-$9 million. She also left sizeable bequests to some of the research staff (but nothing to True) and to many of Bull's other charitable interests. In the midst of the Depression, sums like these were the stuff of fantasy for readers struggling to keep their homes and feed their families.

The story soon assumed the flavour of a melodrama. Mrs. Sidley's son threatened to challenge the will on the grounds of his mother's mental incompetence. Her aged mother died a few days later, a death the newspapers attributed to her shock at losing her daughter.

The Horlick family lawyers challenged the right of the Ontario government to hold an inquest since Mrs. Sidley's body had been buried in the United States, an argument which was expected to establish legal precedent regarding inquests based on forensic samples from a body rather than jurisdictional possession of the body itself . Ontario and Canadian government officials sought to determine what assets Mrs. Sidley held in Canada in hopes of collecting estate taxes. Newspaper accounts positively salivated at the thought that the public purse, so strained by Depression welfare payments, might acquire taxes from the estate of up to $1 million.

The stories made a considerable impact on the public. More than 55 years later, Charlotte Maher, Doris Tucker and Clara Thomas all remembered the case. Charlotte commented that "there was something odd about that [True leaving Perkins Bull]...She wouldn't have liked Sidley staying at Bull's house"; Doris remembered that "I thought he was a scoundrel...There were pages of it. Everybody read it."; and Clara thought that "He was a rascal and a rogue, he really was ferociously strange."

The Bull household came under siege by newspapermen who pursued every car that entered and left, to determine who was inside, and who tried to interview every servant they could contact, past and present. At one point, the succession duties branch of the Treasury Department seized Bull's accounts so he couldn't write cheques. Until his lawyers told him to stop talking to the press, Bull enjoyed the notoriety. One reporter quoted him as smiling as he said, "I pick up a paper or turn on the radio and hear one time I'm worth $10,000,000, another time $3,000,000 and then another story says I'm penniless. It is always very surprising for me to learn these things." He continued, "Many, many things have been published in the press lately, but I won't attempt to comment on those things now. Some of the people are enjoying themselves too much. I won't try to spoil their fun."[33] Not all of it was fun. Bull reported that "I've had dozens of letters ever since this affair began.... Some of the letters have been extremely threatening. Why, they've even threatened to kidnap me in order to get in on the swag."[34]

Many months later the inquest determined that Mrs. Sidley had died of respiratory arrest caused by the atrophy of portions of her brain through disease. Bull came to an arrangement with her son under which he waived his share of the residual estate, keeping only the $250,000 bequest. Bull died ten years later at the age of 78.

When reading newspaper accounts of the inquest, I wondered whether she had asked one of the reporters to note that Bull's secretary, Richard Casson, had replaced, "True Davidson, former secretary of Bull, [who] left his employment early this year."[35] The decision to leave the excitement and challenge of working for Perkins Bull in order to keep house for her parents in Kenilworth may have been taken with difficulty or with relief—there is nothing in her papers to indicate which, although she later expressed resentment that the responsibility of caring for her parents had fallen to her. There is no doubt, however, that she was relieved to be have left the Bull household before she could be associated with what the public interpreted as open scandal and before she had to cope with the months of newspaper frenzy that surrounded the case.

5

TRAGEDY AND THE
STREETSVILLE YEARS
1938–1947

Whatever True's reasons for leaving Bull's employ, and however relieved she must have been not to have been caught up in the media madness that accompanied the inquest into Mrs. Sidley's death, there is little doubt but that she felt trapped by her family obligations and missed the excitement of the business world. Years later, she bitterly told her nephew, Michael, that she felt her sister had abandoned her obligations to help care for their parents, leaving it all up to her. What exactly she expected her sister to do, considering that she was married and living halfway around the world in South Africa, True never told him. Bitterness and resentment are seldom rational and True doubtless felt relieved to have a family member to whom she could finally vent her feelings about this period. She cared deeply for her parents and, however imprisoned and cheated she may have felt by the need to care for them, she had too strong a sense of family responsibility to fail them when they needed her.

Rev. Davidson served as a supply minister in Kenilworth from 1938 to 1940. True ran the household, wrote and submitted more magazine stories and articles and, in 1940, ran as an unsuccessful candidate for the C.C.F. In 1940, her father retired and purchased an old house in Streetsville on which he commissioned considerable upgrading work. True intended to commute from there to Toronto for work.

During the move to Streetsville, there was a traffic accident. True later described how she was driving and trying to catch up to the moving van. "I don't know. The tires were old. And perhaps I was driving too fast. Anyway we had a blowout. The car swayed and then it went on its side. The marble clock was too delicate to pack and when the car turned on its side the clock fell on my father's neck."[1] He died four days later on July 10th. "He left me with my mother who was an invalid and in a situation which was just disastrous. My father said to me before he died: 'Now don't become disheartened if things are hard for a while. One door never closes but another door opens.'"[2]

True mourned her father for a long time. She had already begun her custom of writing a poem for her Christmas/New Years cards. Her 1941 Christmas poem eloquently expressed her sense of loss and search for recovery.

Grey Thoughts on a Green Christmas

What does Christmas say
To the shivering earth,
Wet and cold and grey,
Stripped of love and mirth.

....

But give the heart to grief,
And it will float as light
As a summer-fallen leaf
On a dark stream at night.

Loose the tensioned will—
Hope and fear depart,
Leaving peace a still
Sweetness in the heart.[3]

True completed the move into the Streetsville house with her mother and oversaw completion of the renovations. Harry Evans, who was about eight years old when True moved to Streetsville, remembered the house well. "...the bloody house was terrible...it was the perfect haunted house...it was grey clapboard that had shutters that banged in the breeze and there was a tree out front that had grown into the house...and the sidewalk and the street-light would be loose and the shadows through the tree...She kept cats, there was an abandoned well and an old orchard in the back full of grotesque trees and an old barn." He also said that "it was a very old house, from prior to 1900." His older brother, Garfield, also remembered the house writing that "to us kids the house was haunted and had been for some time...of course the place had to be wired up. So Charlie Evans (dad) and helper Garf (10 yrs old) were called in....The house was [also] having its first bathroom in-stalled. Plumbers, carpenters, electricians, even a bricklayer point-ing up chimney cracks."[4] Garfield also remembered receiving "the scare of [his] life" while working on the house.

> Dad sent me down to the dark basement with a flashlight for some-thing or other (loose wires) and part way up the cellar steps I met an old woman with 2 big black eyes (shiners) snow white hair and she was laughing. Holy smoke. Big hooked nose looking at one scared kid. It was True's mother. I found out an 1/2 hour later what it was all about. Mother & daughter had been in a car accident. No seat belts in those days and the dear old soul had whacked the dash-board."[5]

Harry remembered that True and her mother were dressed in a very old-fashioned way. "Her hair...the dresses they wore, the colours they wore...were just like something out of Dickens." He also recalled that "the old girl, her mother, dear soul, her breath was like death, she was bedridden and she could scarcely get around and she smelled of death to me."

True must have already been known and respected in the Streetsville, then only a village, described by Harry Evans as hav-ing "900 people, including dogs and cats." Garfield Evans recalled True calling her father up to the half-installed bathroom while they were installing the electricity.

> "I hear dad start to laugh and then True. I have a look in the bath-room and True is in the tub sitting down. She has a piece of white chalk and she is saying "I want a light right here." The old man says, "No can't do that." "Why Not." Well the inspection dept. OHEPC says no outlets or even light switches in the bathroom. So dad phones

Harry Pichard, the inspector, at dinner time to plead the case. When
he heard who it was for he okayed it along with some special instructions and he wanted to see the whole set up before the walls were
sealed up. So True got her light to read by in the bathtub."[6]

True soon got a job in Toronto writing articles for the Board of
Trade *Journal.* Joan Moore wrote that she remembered True well
from that time. True took the train to and from work and Moore
wrote, "One incidence I remember quite clearly involves the train.
As True had not been working she did not have a very large
wardrobe and each day she would delve into an old trunk and pull
out something to wear. The lengths of dresses then as now were
always changing and many of True's clothes were too long. One
day she decided to shorten the dress on the way to work and she
arrived at the office with only half the hem completed. This did
not bother her in the least."[7] She recalled another incident when
True was going out to do an interview for an article and their boss
said "True, please put in your teeth and your slip is showing."
"She just smiled."

She also remembered True telling fortunes with sticks, "she
would always see such terrible things happening. As my boyfriend
was overseas I never wanted her to tell mine." She concluded that
remembered True as " a great down to earth person who did not
put on airs and did her job to the best of her ability."

In April 1941, True was appointed Clerk and Treasurer of the
Village of Streetsville and Secretary of the Public Utilities Commission, during the absence of the clerk, Captain J.W. Drennan,
who had been called to active military service.[8] *The Streetsville
Review* wrote that "she has had considerable experience in clerical work and we believe she will fill the position with satisfaction."[9]True herself said that she only got the job because the people in the village knew she needed it.

> I didn't know anything about book-keeping or records or anything
> of that sort. I was quite outside my field....So that field opened for
> me and I took mother in an invalid chair down to the office with me
> and she sat and happily read aloud to me while I did my work. I
> wonder where in the city you could have had a job in which a
> woman sat and read the whole of Wells' Outline of History to you
> while you were keeping your books. But nobody commented on it in

Streetsville. Mother was happy. She was entertaining me and I was happy because she was entertained. You never forget a small town that does something like that for you."[10]

Harry Evans didn't remember any discussion about giving True the job out of charity. "True, to me, wasn't someone who needed sympathy." He described "going to Council Meetings and her sitting there very business-like, with a pad and pencil taking the notes and so on and extremely disciplined, and typing in the office and, boy, you didn't cross her up...she was really in charge of the place." His brother Garfield remembered her as "well built with a straight back and a ready smile. She usually wore a black suit cut just below the knees and a white blouse. Her hat was black and jaunty with a small feather." He also told how his father "was Chairman of the Public School Board and when he came home after a meeting he would hold forth on how the world needed more women like True. OK, she had her enemies. Some women were green eyed, no doubt about that."[11] When told of this, Doris Tucker responded that True "wouldn't stop from doing something just because ladies didn't do that. If she thought it was in the interest of her or someone else, she'd go right ahead. And if they baulked her, that would just make her more determined."

True continued to work at these two nearly full-time jobs until at least 1944, travelling to Toronto by train to her job at the Board of Trade most weekdays and taking the minutes at the Council and Public Utilities meetings in the evenings. Harry Evans remembers True as the village eccentric.

I always had a sense of adventure with True... she was unique, a self-made woman like...I think there were attempts to court her...my father was quite a rogue. I can say this now that he is gone. He would be the type that would buy True a bottle of wine, but of course, True would have nothing to do with that...but my father was a real joker. He would do things like that just for the devilment...to get her goat. Dad was on the Town Utilities...he and True crossed swords at one time or another and this would be my father's way of getting back at her...she was definitely talked about...she didn't really fit in because she could do anything....I don't recall any serious beaux. That would have been most interesting to me. But I don't recall any, other, of course, than married men and that would be part of the reason, I guess, the women would talk about her. Because a single woman, in those days, alone with a man was a no-no. You just didn't do that. But True, frankly, didn't give a damn. She'd go where she liked, when she liked and how she liked...She'd be a tough woman for a guy to handle.

When True wasn't working she was out most evenings at the drama club, poetry readings and other social activities. She sponsored several prizes for the Streetsville Fair including the best "Historical Map of Streetsville and Environs," "Objects of Historical Interest," and the best "Historical Short Story."[12]

It was through the drama club that Harry Evans got to know her best. "When she needed a kid for the play, as a slave boy, I was it. On one memorable occasion, True was supposed to be something in the play, but she'd broken her leg or something, so she did a monologue while they changed the scenes. She came out in her chair and the curtain opened up. I was fascinated by this lady, the guts she had."

She soon hired him to clean the ashes out of the furnace. He described her house as "terrible...I think there was indoor plumbing but the...bathroom was the sort of place you wouldn't stay too long. The house, I think if you walked, the dust would rise. She was not a housekeeper. Or a cook. The smells just used to...well you know...it was real old house...there were one or two rooms that they lived in, an old back kitchen kind of thing [and] an old, old furnace in the basement and when you'd sift the ashes in the basement the dust would go right up through the house." Joan Moore remembered having dinner at True's home in Streetsville one time and "while we were sitting in the dining room eating, her cat had kittens there."[13] It is amusing and perhaps revealing that among the clippings True saved was the following poem:

> Housekeeping is, say many men,
> A snap. There's nothing to it.
> They mean, of course, housekeeping when
> Some woman's there to do it.[14]

True appears to have kept her political allegiances quiet during her years in Streetsville. Harry Evans was surprised to hear that she had been a member of the C.C.F. and commented that "that would be another thing that would go against her. In Streetsville there were two parties, there were the Tories and the Grits. God help anyone else, being CCF would not make her popular about there at all."

One of the short stories True published during these years was one in *The New Outlook,* which so resembled the story of her life that it might be safe to read into it some of her own feelings of entrapment and fears of never escaping back to the excitement of the city. In this story, True's heroine dreams of going to the city . She is intelligent, works hard and saves enough money to do so, but on the day that she is to leave, she startles the horse which bolts, killing her father and seriously injuring her mother. She is forced to remain in the village to take care of her mother and when a sympathetic local boy asks her to marry him, she is so lonely that she accepts. Although they have a good marriage and nine children, she never forgets her dream. The story ends, in a highly dramatic (and unrealistic fashion), with True's heroine dying of a brain fever brought on by her disappointments.[15] True certainly didn't expect to die of a "brain-fever" because she had to look after her mother, but she shared much of her heroine's sense of entrapment. One of True's more touching poems may been drawn from an incident with her mother. In it she recalls speaking "harshly to a loved one, without thought,"

> And I quickly kissed the shocked surprise
> From the dear querulous mouth and puzzled eyes,
> Turned back the question with quick soft laughter.
> And went back to my work refreshed.
> We do what is given us to do in mansion or in hovel.[16]

True nursed her mother until she died. Around the same time the Village Clerk returned from military service and True's job in Streetsville ended. Lonely, depressed and ill, she sold the Streetsville house and bought a small house in East York. She was at her lowest ebb. Little did she know that the best years of her life were just about to begin!

6

BEGINNING A NEW LIFE IN

EAST YORK

1947–1958

Twenty Years a Chief

*T*rue didn't know it when she moved to East York in 1947, but her years as a warrior had ended, and her "20 years a chief" were about to begin. There was certainly nothing to indicate that her situation was about to improve so dramatically. She was deeply depressed and lonely after her mother's death, telling a reporter later that "After my mother's death there seemed to be no point in life. There was a period when I would come home and not bother to turn on the heat or cook a meal or anything."[1] She was broke and struggling to make a living writing for magazines. Then her doctor sent to Princess Margaret Hospital with a tentative diagnosis of cancer. "She had the symptoms, but ...True didn't have cancer. She [just] thought life was no longer worth living."[2] Emily Smith, who met True shortly after she moved to East York and remained a close friend until her death, said that True didn't say much about this diagnosis. "She kept things pretty close to her chest, you know. She was very self-controlled and she wasn't publicizing her problems. She fought all her own problems. She was really a Stoic, I think."

True exhausted her inheritance from the sale of the house in Streetsville when she bought a three-room cottage on Linsmore Crescent in East York which she later described as "a combination egg-crate."[3] She added a bathroom and a back porch with "enough insulation so I wouldn't freeze when I had a bath."[4] Emily Smith remembered it as a "little house...you could hardly get anybody in it...you just go from one room to another...just a little wee house...she didn't keep a very tidy house, but she knew where everything was." Doris Tucker remembered it having only "about two rooms. A terrible place." True's neighbour, Gord Hazlett, agreed with her description of it as a chicken coop. "That name sure fit at that time as it was about 12' wide and maybe 30' long. 1 storey, no basement. Since then two rooms have been added to the rear and a part basement dug."[5]

True had not intended staying in East York when she moved there, but the friendly neighbours soon changed her mind. While she was unpacking, her two cats scampered up a tree and "within minutes the neighbours gathered around advising her on how to get the pets down."..."And they talk about communities being cold and unfriendly!"[6] Even better, the street was full of children, and they soon drew her out of her depression. She said of this time that:

> The street was full of children. Small houses usually have big families. I don't know why this is. And I loved them. I always have been a pushover for children. Anyway when the kids went back to school I saw all these big kids who were still around on the streets and they still kept visiting me and taking all my time.
>
> So I said, "Right, everyone who's coming to see me comes between the hours of 9:30 and 11 or 10 and 12 or whatever it was." So this developed into a little kindergarten. I bought plasticine and crayons and whatever supplies I could think of. It developed into a fair size kindergarten."[7]

Emily Smith recalled that "she had the children organized down there and was giving them a good education." Gord Hazlett wrote that "True was a very good neighbour to have. The children just adored her. She would have them in her yard or front porch and I believe tell them stories. Sometimes they sang songs." Doris Tucker didn't know True at that time but could imagine how she came to run a kindergarten. "Those houses on Linsmore were all individually built and the people in them really suffered in the Depression and I guess she thought 'Well, they don't have a kindergarten so I guess I'll help.'"

Once again involved in something she believed worthwhile, True's health and morale improved. Her kindergarten was so successful that the neighbours urged her to run for the local school board to push for kindergartens for all of the children in East York. She told reporters later, that since she was "down and out and it seemed nothing more could happen to her,"[8] and she expected to only be alive for a year, that she decided that she "could do jolly well as I pleased for that year."[9] Jack Christie, who later served on Council and the Hydro Commission with True, laughed when I told him that she had written about being pushed into running for the School Board. "Nobody pushed True Davidson into anything. But she was always the sort of person who gets involved in things and if someone said 'you should go on School Board to make that happen' she would probably do so."[10] Clara Thomas agreed. "I can't believe that anything like that ever happened to True that way, by chance. I think she had her eye on that kind of advancement. Always. Always." True later wrote that "If you are meant to take control/In any circle of life in which you find yourself/It will be forced on you."[11]

It is said that when Agnes MacPhail arrived in Ottawa in 1922 as Canada's first female M.P., that she "was as welcome as an unexpected guest at a dinner party. Colleagues in the House of Commons hoped she would go away or, if not, sit quietly in a corner."[12] True's reception on the School Board wasn't much warmer. In a speech given to the Junior Board of Trade in 1968 she recounted that she was ignored by her male colleagues at the first school board meeting "who thought women should know their place—which wasn't on the school board of East York. True was doubly unsuitable in the minds of the men on the school board—not only was she a woman, she was also a member of the C.C.F. *The Toronto Star* later wrote that "staid, conservative members of the board regarded her candidacy with the same distaste afforded carriers of bubonic plague."[13] But acceptance finally came, at lunch during an educational trip, when she admitted she preferred beer to sherry and would just as soon have both."[14]

True never sat in the corner and kept quiet. As one account

put it: "she…fought for East York and its inhabitants with a ferocity that swamps her political foes and bemuses her colleagues …"[15] Within two years, East York had a kindergarten programme "renting whatever extra space required."[16] She began to fight for special classes for "…the hard-of-hearing, the retarded, the rapid learners" and for "bigger playgrounds, instrumental music and better library facilities."[17] She felt strongly that Canada had its own literature and that the schools should be teaching more of it. In his tribute at her funeral, Dalton A. Morrison, then Director of Education for East York said:

> True's mark is on this community's educational development. She pushed for programs to recognize individual differences…academic excellence…music and the arts…scholarship fund…student government…improved educational climate…competitive working conditions for staff…library resource centres…trustee workshops…In educational circles it has been said that women are overlooked. True broke this mould in 1952 to become the first woman to chair the East York Board of Education and again to chair the finance committee of the Metropolitan School Board.[18]

She disagreed vehemently with the school board's Chairman, George Webster, whom she quoted as telling the township's secondary school teachers: "We don't want Scholarship winners in this sytem. We just want good, all-round boys and girls."[19] True firmly believed that students should be challenged to excel. This, however, did not mean that she believed in coddling them. She said "there is such a thing as healthy poverty for children," and that while she didn't believe in cold, calculated punishment she was not opposed to spur-of-the-moment discipline."[20] As one of her obituaries noted, "As often as not, her losing causes became better known than her rivals' winning causes. Once, she urged Metro to provide "wild playgrounds" where kids would be urged to break things and "come to grips with nature in the raw."[21]

Having found a new calling to satisfy her, she threw herself into it wholeheartedly—and into a myriad of other activities. She attended a trustee's workshop at the University of Michigan in 1949 and worked as superintendent of the Bolton Camp for two summers. She became a very active member of the local dramatic club. Since a trustee's stipend wasn't enough to live on, she continued to write magazine articles and short stories. She also resumed active involvement in the CCF , serving on the provincial education committee. Within two years, she had worked herself into a state of complete exhaustion. She wrote to her friend, Emily Smith, in August 1950 that:

...I have got so bogged down with things I had to do or ought to do or just simply wanted to do, that I haven't been able to do anything....

> This is something that happens to me periodically. In an excess of enthusiasm I take on various business business and social duties, to which I have recently added a wide variety of absolutely new fields while resolutely refusing to drop any of the old ones. You know that I have not had more than two or three weeknights free between New Year's Day and Dominion Day, and those by accident, while my weekends were usually full also. I have often gone to two or three meetings in one night. Well, this camel's back doesn't break, but the last straw makes it sag to a pitiable concavity, and when a camel's back becomes concave instead of convex, progress is no longer possible. It simply lies down. The vacation school was the last straw. I simply lay down. I was so tired I would have to sit down two or three times to rest my arms in the course of doing my hair. Iwas so tired I wanted to sleep instead of eat...I didn't write to my cousin who was going to be in town and wanted to see me. I didn't get my bankbook made up and got my account overdrawn although I had a couple of hundred dollars due me for work I had turned in before the "Great Sleep" but hadn't got around to collecting. In short I was a mess.[22]

Exhausted though she may have been, True was never happier. As soon as she recovered from the "Great Sleep" she resumed her old activities and added more. As she later wrote, she was on the School Board when it "couldn't keep up with the flood of children. [We] were putting additions on new schools before the original buildings were fully occupied."[23] She was elected in time for the completion of Cosburn and of St. Clair Jr. High Schools and the building of Victoria Park, Presteign Heights, Selwyn, George Webster and Parkside. True talked with amusement of the story submitted by a Grade 6 student at Presteign Heights in response to a prize she had offered for the best tall story, "...little Sharon Martin was the winner, with a story of the extension of the school in successive leaps until it reached the Orange Crush plant and they were able to roller skate along the halls for a drink at noon break."[24]

Elected Chairman of the Board of Education in 1952, Dalton Morrison recalled that "...True broke every known convention, leaving friends, colleagues and others gasping. No chairman, before or since, met me at six o'clock, a.m. True had an exceptional

Township of East York, Board of Education, 1953. *Courtesy the Todmorden Mills Heritage Museum and Arts Centre*

command of parliamentary procedure in chairmanship. When she forgot a rule, which was rare...she made her own, unchallenged....If it is to be, it's up to me. This [was] True's message. When there's a job to be done, some say, "Let George do it." ...True Davidson put it this way..."Here am I, send me."[25] During her years as Chairman of the East York Board she also served as President of the Ontario School Trustees and Ratepayers (Urban Section), as Chairman of the Canadian School Trustees Committee on French in Elementary Schools and as Finance Chairman of the Metropolitan Toronto School Board. She also

took an unusually active classroom role for a trustee. Helen
Juhola, who grew up in East York, remembered her childhood impression of True as "this wierd woman who came to everything,
always wearing a different hat."[26] She published poems to the students in the school newsletters.[27] Charlotte Maher remembered
her talking "about taking trips with the kids when she was on the
Board of Education which was kind of an odd thing for a trustee
to do —but maybe it was different then—and enjoying it, and trying to stretch the opportunities for kids to learn."

She was actively involved with the University Women's Club,
Woodbine United Church, and the East York Literature Group, to
whom she was quoted as saying:

> It makes me angry to hear a first-rate poet like Earl Birney writing a
> case-history of Canada as a schizophrenic adolescent. We have con-
> flicts in Canada certainly, but psychologists assure us that it is re-
> pression which makes conflicts really dangerous, and there is no re-
> pression here. Minorities are permitted and even encouraged to re-
> tain their characteristics and customs. Indeed, if the U.S. is the
> world's melting-pot, Canada may well be called its preserving ket-
> tle...Canada is unique in many ways...It was created and survived
> in almost direct defiance of the laws of geographic and economic
> determinism. The tendency in Canada is toward mutual understand-
> ing and respect. Far from apologizing for Canada as an immature
> country with an inferiority complex or a split personality, we should
> be proud of the rather wise, just, kindly, tolerant and essentially adult
> civilization which it seems to be evolving.[28]

She discussed the same theme in a series of ten lectures she taught
at Woodsworth House around this time. The lectures reviewed the
factors "in our physical and international environment and historical and economic development which have coloured our thinking
and helped at once to create and to solve our problems."[29] She
would likely be disappointed to learn that Canadians are still asking the same questions that she posed in the introduction of her
flyer about this cours—"People once thought the Dominion of
Canada a wild idea that could never work. Were they right? Are
we a nation or just a collection of immature and mutually distrust-
ful provinces? Have we won political freedom from Britain only to
become an economic and cultural colony of the U.S.?"

True also busy working with the C.C.F. She edited their publication, *CCF News*,[30] and ran twice as a the provincial C.C.F. in the riding of York East. York East had a tradition of political activism. Doris Tucker remembered that "everybody felt akin to the CCF then because everyone was so hard up. I never joined but I went to hear them." This activism grew from the grim conditions endured by the primarily working-class residents of the community during the Depression. True recalled hearing from one resident "of taking a layette to a fam-

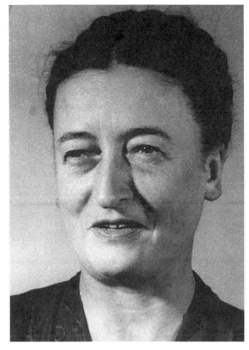

Photograph of True taken when she was running for the provincial CCF in York East. *Courtesy Emily Smith*

ily where she found the new baby wrapped in newspaper. There were reports of other babies lying dead on the dump near Goodwood Park Crescent, or on the land north of Toronto East General Hospital because there was no money to bury them."[31] The East York Worker's Association became the largest and most successful of the workers' organizations in Toronto during the Depression, seeking to find jobs and to protect the living standards of relief recipients. In 1935, they organized a strike by 2700 families in reaction to a proposed cut in welfare. Doris Tucker was among the employees escorted out of the municipal building by police when it was stormed and occupied by the Workers' Association. Women in the association established a Parents' Clinic in 1936 to distribute birth control supplies with the relief allotments, arguing that womens' freedom was intrinsically tied to their control of reproduction. True recalled that "At the time, the *East York Weekly News* carried an editorial demanding, "Which is the greater sin, to steal or to see your loved ones starve?"[32] In 1934, Arthur

Williams, described by True as "a Welsh-born orator—said to have a voice to charm the birds off the trees and charisma to burn"[33] was elected briefly as Reeve. Later, he became the CCF member of Parliament for the Ontario Riding where his eloquence continued to attract him considerable attention.[34] True wrote that the inevitable "talk of Communist infiltration" eventually caused moderate supporters like John Hollinger to quietly withdraw but "the Communist fringe never gained control" and the "organization...affiliated with the C.C.F."[35] York East's C.C.F. support remained strong enough to ensure the election of Agnes MacPhail as their provincial representative in 1943 and 1946.[36] True knew and greatly respected both Agnes MacPhail and Arthur Williams and had worked with both during the 1930s while she was employed by Perkins Bull. Her decision to move to the Township may well have been influenced by their association with it.

But the glory days for the CCF in East York were over by the time True became their representative. In 1971 she said "I ran for the CCF 15 or 16 years ago when the CCF had fallen on very stony places. I don't know why I ran. I had no thought of winning."[37] The years immediately after W.W.II were a bad time for the party. As Walter Young wrote:

> Most Canadians were unwilling to see business, profits, and competition as evils, and were unmoved by the educational activities of the CCF. Those who were victims of capitalism often viewed their misfortune as simply the luck of the game. The CCF assumed the existence of a Canadian working class. Objectively, such a class existed, but the members of that class did not, for the most part, accept their position as such. Their aspirations and attitudes were middle class.[38]

Despite knowing that she stood almost no chance of being elected, True threw herself into these campaigns with all of her characteristic energy. The *York East CCF News* recorded that "In the fortnight since nomination, our new federal candidate has attended the following functions: a church luncheon at which she was a guest speaker, a Neighbourhood Workers' luncheon, a luncheon for some of her own campaign volunteers, a Home and School Meeting at which she spoke, two school concerts at one of which she spoke, the two-day CCF Youth Convention at which she was a fraternal delegate, the two-day Provincial Council, and several church meetings, as well as the regular Monday CCF meetings."[39] A killing pace indeed, but as she was later quoted as saying: "There will come for all of us a dawn that we shall not see, but let none of those who loved us then say, 'What a pity she drove herself so hard.' Say rather, 'There went one of the fortunate ones, who lived every moment until she died.'"[40]

Nina Roberts and her late husband, Bill, got to know True Davidson around this time since they attended the same church. Nina helped True with one of her campaigns for the CCF and told me that:

> I can well remember one of the sessions we had for the CCF that she was losing badly. She came back to the committee room and she said to me, "How many did I get?" and I told her and she just stood there. Oh, I could have bawled! I almost had to leave the place, it was just so awful. And she had worked so hard, I don't think she'd been eating, and I just couldn't stay...[41]

True lost both campaigns, running a poor third. As Doris Tucker commented, "when you're running for an election you're surrounded by your own people. You don't really know what's going on on the outside. It must have been hard for her to lose."

What doubtless made it even more difficult were True's growing personal doubts about the direction in which her party was heading. Her primary inspiration, J.S. Woodsworth, was gone. Agnes MacPhail was gone. A new group were in charge. Martin Lipset wrote of them that "the newer and younger socialists who joined a going movement wanted power and proceeded to try and get it."[42] True, who had admired Woodsworth's principled demand for being right rather than politic, was uncomfortable within the more disciplined party structure. Walter Young described members like her when he wrote: "Success, they feared would transform the CCF from a vehicle of protest into a disciplined party in which there would be little room for the rebel."[43] Doris Tucker remembered the CCF as having "a very strong philosophy. Woodsworth was the dreamer in a sense...They were really smart men but it was more than just politics with them, you know. But, I guess, maybe that was why she was in it but then when she got the down-to-earth types in, where all they could think of was getting elected and running the municipality on CCF lines...she wouldn't like that."

In 1954, True walked out of a Toronto area party conference that called on members to run municipally on a party label. "She said party politics should be kept out of municipal councils, and as she became more immersed in municipal politics, she drifted away from her party involvement."[44] She was uncomfortable also with the growing involvement of labour unions in the party and later refused to join the NDP because of its partnership with them, writing that "I never joined the NDP. I didn't like the NDP from its beginning. I came to believe that socialism wouldn't cure the ills of the world. I couldn't see it."[45] Although she supported many social measures for the underprivileged, True came to believe that "governments could often go too far in propping people up and not letting them feel the rough hand of experience as she herself had done. It won't hurt school kids to learn that life is not an endless handout, she often said. "It's no fun," she once recalled, "drawing unemployment insurance cheques and walking the streets trying to find a job.... She sided with the downtrodden. But those she felt were shiftless got no sympathy."[46] Her anger was greatest towards those who she felt failed people by encouraging them to be avoid the struggles and rewards of hard work. Her belief that people needed to work for a living in order to maintain their self-respect provided the theme for her poem, "Leisure," part of which appears below.

> I am not going to work today;
> I shall sit on the front steps and drink beer;
> The work ethic is outmoded anyway. ...
> We are on strike. We have disrupted the entire economy of the country,
> but we have no reason to be troubled, ...
> We will go back to work next week or next month or sometime and our wages will be doubled.
> If the plant has to close, there's still unemployment insurance or welfare to look after our pay,
> We will always be supported;
> In fact we will be courted
> Whenever a municipal or provincial or federal election is near.
>
> Inside, I hate myself.[47]

True's decision to abandon her party allegiance did not occur without considerable soul-searching and regret. In 1971 she told a reporter that "the CCF was very good to me and I have no grudge at all. I just wished I could have continued to support them."[48] Among her clippings was part of a poem which questioned the Communist party, likely kept because it expressed her own feelings about her allegiances.

The party is a clear well, but does that mean
that I should no longer wash myself?
The party is a powerful rock—
but am I therefore only a speck of dust,
condemned to impotence.
The party is the brain of our class—
Am I therefore not allowed to have opinions of my own?
The party is always in the right
But the man at the top:
Is he also always in the right?
The party is a monolith, surely,
But am I therefore a renegade
everytime when I am in doubt?[49]

Having decided to leave the party of her youthful dedication, True became equally dedicated to their opposition. While she objected most strongly to the union connection, she also rejected their support of democratic socialism, later criticizing David Lewis as "a doctrinaire socialist, fettered by self-regarding trade unions. He could not admit, even to himself, that democratic socialism leads to disaster."[50]

Throughout all this time True still had to try to make a living —and she did it poorly. Her stipend as a trustee was only an honorarium; her writing didn't bring in enough to live on; and when she went to employment agencies she said that they "referred me to jobs I couldn't possibly have taken...They kept suggesting me for stenography and secretarial jobs. I would pity the boss who would hire me as a stenographer because I would be correcting his grammar and spelling and rewriting his letters."[51]In the midst of all this, her sister returned to Canada, dying of cancer soon after her arrival. True's nephews never understood why their mother had chosen to leave them and their father when she was faced

with death, but Doris Tucker, from her knowledge of True, suspected that her sister felt that "she was not in her country. I guess
she had to come home to die."

Emily Smith talked about how "True never had any money.
She managed so many things so well for a person who had as little
money as she had....She made do with more things than I ever
knew anybody to. I didn't know that kind of—I was going to
say—poverty. It was poverty." After True sold her little house on
Linsmore she "moved several places, paying rent. She really had to
have a very low rent rate in order to have a place of her own. For
awhile she lived here in our recreation room. It was always a matter of being able to pay the rent." Jack Christie remembered True
"living in a basement apartment on Cosburn Avenue and other
than her bed all her furniture was orange crates covered in fabric"
and that "she never had much money. Half the time she was on
the Hydro Commission she was behind in her rates." Willis Blair
recalled that "True was frugal in every way. She had to be. She
had no money. When she'd go to school board conventions—she
went to every one she could—she'd take the money that was required for train fare or plane fare, whatever, and she'd take a
cheaper route and use the difference to eat on."[52] In a letter to
Emily Smith in 1950 True wryly mentioned that "I have had out
an abscessed tooth that has been quietly decaying for the past six
months, and have promised the dentist that I will have a whole
raft more out...soon...I plan also to have one or two little things
put right inside me to which an intelligent person would have attended long ago, and in some way I have to finance all this reckless
extravagance, so I guess as far as my holidays for this summer are
concerned I've had them ..."[53]

In some ways True was better off not having to maintain a
home during those years. She was too busy to properly maintain
a house on her own and she couldn't afford to hire help. Gord
Hazlett remembered that "she was never one to cut her grass in
the back yard and I can remember her sitting among the tall grass
with shorts & halter eating something out of a bowl and giving
her dog Yo-Yo and cat the odd sample. Yo Yo was an unruly
cocker spaniel and when True came out at night, maybe 11 p.m.,
to call Yo Yo for bed she could be heard as far away as Coxwell
and Greenwood. I think Yo Yo was out electioneering for his
master."

Dressing well was impossible on such a limited income although True always loved nice clothes. Lorraine Hazlett recalled that True seemed to be always going up or down Linsmore with dress or hat boxes before she was supposed to take part in a public function and wondered whether she had to borrow her wardrobe. Emily Smith said that "I imagine a lot of people were critical [about how she dressed.] She had such a personality that...she managed the best of everything that could be possible with as little as possible ..." Among True's many clippings was a rather unlikely one entitled "Secrets of Charm" which advocated settling "an unbreakable date" each day for some aspect of grooming and assured its readers that "By setting a schedule rigidly, you'll find that you can display your appearance to its best advantage seven days a week...To be always ready to go anywhere; do anything; knowing at all times that you will be looking your best, will give you the poise that is the basic requirement of charm. You will be unhurried, unflurried and free to give your entire attention to the pleasures of the moment."[54] True never seemed to be able to achieve this. Doris Tucker tells a story about a time when True was late in getting ready for a public event and "she came out of her house with her long hair still wet and she leaned out of the car window all along the way so that the wind would dry it in time."

Doris also remembered some of the gossip that circulated about True. Sometimes, she said, they talked about how she dressed and sometimes "they thought she drank too much in the early years but she stopped that. She'd take one glass and hold it all evening. She had to keep her wits about her too because people were always approaching her about some problem or other." But she never remembered any gossip about True and men, a statement backed by Gord Hazlett who wrote that "she sure didn't lead an immoral life as any men visiting her place were never allowed in the house and she spoke to them at length on her verandah."

For a few years during this time, True taught at the Hillfield Private School in Hamilton, travelling there each day by bus. While there she organized a newsletter, called *The Hillfield Piglet*, of short stories and poetry "published from time to time by 5B and 4A." Although all the material was supposedly written by the students, one poem was obviously written by True and shows us her picture of herself as a teacher.

She sits on the desk, though a master stands;
She bats her eyes and waggles her hands;
She can't play soccer or give you the strap;
She looks as if she needed a nine-years nap;
When she talks about poetry her old eyes gleam
Like a boy with seven hidden plates of pink ice cream;
In a funny way she likes us, but she makes a lot of fuss
About things that are almost incomprehensible to us;
She thinks that teaching shouldn't be a battle or a game;
She loves to study English, and wants us to feel the same;
She's hurt if we don't listen, and when we disobey
It nearly drives her crazy, which she's almost anyway;
Its been stimulating in a way, but very puzzling too,
For she treats men as her equals, which no woman ought to do;
Still, its been most interesting; we'll remember it with glee;
And describe it most amusingly
And so will she.[55]

True was never a "technical" teacher although Clara Thomas told me that she was interested in the theories of education and Emily Smith first met True because some of the creative teaching activities that her Emily's husband, Lorne, had initiated at East York Collegiate. True taught mostly from her own knowledge and inspired by her enthusiasm. In 1971 she criticized the Ontario Institute for Studies in Education, charging that it was "made up of American professors who got their degrees in education and not in any area of scholarship" and that she was concerned because "our school system is dominated by those who have been educated by American educators."[56] That same year she told the Toronto Businessmen's Liberal Club that "knowledge of the education process was not necessarily important to teaching and it would be better for teachers to be trained in the subject they will teach."

True enjoyed teaching at Hillfield School and the income was a help, but the long commute was exhausting. It was likely a relief, when she was elected to East York Council, in 1958, and decided to resign from teaching to dedicate herself full-time to her new position.

7

THE GHOST AND MISS DAVIDSON

1958–1962

*T*rue topped the polls in her first run for Council, receiving 5,772 votes out of a possible 40,000. Her nearest competitor was more than 600 votes behind. She enthused to the reporters that "It's unbelievable, it's wonderful. I'll serve 10 years on council like the last 10 years I had on the Board of Education." She spoke of how she had decided to run because it was time for a change and because she believed that East York needed a master plan of zoning bylaws. "East York should have planned development such as they have in European cities. We are small, compact and cohesive, and we could do a planning job that could be the envy of Canada."[1] Her decision to run certainly wasn't for the money. Willis Blair, elected that same year, remembered that "we got $1,450 for our first year on Council"—although, even this sum was more than what True had been receiving as a school board trustee.

Although settlement in the East York area can be traced back to the 1790s, the municipality itself was only thirty-four years old when True joined Council. As True later wrote, East York "was hardly old enough to be well established in 1929 when we entered the chill days of depression. Growth was impossible and even hope was hard to maintain. Only after blood was pumped back into the veins of our economy by the terrible surgical processes of war did we become what from the beginning we had in us to be." She described the members of Council in those days as "individual giants" who ran things their way, but who ran them well. "I remember coming home from the Annex area of Toronto one snowy night when the Bloor cars were running a stub line along the single cleared track. I crossed hopelessly to the Hollinger bus depot, and found to my amazement, East York's buses buzzing merrily backwards and forewards along fully cleared highways. Of course, John Hollinger was on Council." She said that "the Kiwanians ran East York in those days. Bill Heaton and Percy Muir ruled the elected officials with a firm hand. Walter Stewart built libraries out of nothing with the help of the Kiwanians and collected paintings of A.Y. Jackson...George Curtis and Wilf Turner strove mightily in the interests of music, and Norman Tuckwell's Collegiate orchestra...started many able students on the way to musical excellence."[2]

In her first term on Council, True became Chairman of the Works Committee and began agitating to dispose of some of the unnecessary land owned by the municipality which she described as "a liability to us in their present condition."[3] When she became Reeve in 1960 she followed through on this idea, deeding 245 acres of valley land to the Metropolitan Toronto and Region Conservation Authority as part of its flood control and water conservation scheme. The local paper claimed that this was the largest single block of land ever donated to the Authority by a member-municipality.[4] Willis Blair approved since East York, with a population of only 72,000, couldn't afford to develop the land into parks.

Another of her early contributions to the municipality was the creation of the Dominion Day celebrations. This was one of Jack Christie's first experiences with True. He remembered that the Reeve, Jack Allen, opposed the idea, saying "who's going to stay in town on Dominion Day for a little parade? But True never did give up. She demanded that it happen and it did." Jack Christie believes that East York had the first Dominion Day parade in Metropolitan Toronto, a claim also made by True. She took equal pride in her establishment of the Simcoe Day celebrations. "We led the way with Simcoe Day celebrations also, and this example, too, is being followed elsewhere."[5] Doris Tucker remembered that it was through True's prompting that "we started celebrating Dominion Day on a grand scale. In my recollection a great deal of planning went into this project under the enthusiastic efforts of both the Recreation Director...and [True.] The celebration was a day long event, starting off with a parade...followed by official opening ceremonies...then entertainment, and athletic contests, etc.

Contingent of firefighters led by their colour guard at the corner of Woodbine and Lumsden Ave., marching in the Dominion Day Parade. During her first term in office, True started East York's annual Dominion Day Parade. The Reeve at the time said that "no one would come. They'd all be at their cottages_ but it has continued as one of the major annual public events in East York. *Courtesy the East York Fire Department*

throughout the day. In the evening there was dancing under the stars...followed by the grand finale, which was a beautiful display of fireworks. The parade...was always quite an attraction with its bands, decorated floats and many marching groups...The Reeve rode in a special car near the front of the parade. For the occasion [True] wore a new outfit, topped by a very stunning wide brimmed hat....As far as I can recall during True's regime every Dominion Day was treated to the sight of True in another special outfit."

The good weather enjoyed by the Dominion Day Parade became part of the True Davidson myth in East York. Jack Christie remembered that "there has never been enough rain to get in the way of the event but...the year after True died he went down to the park where the parade was assembling and it was raining and it looked like it was going to get worse. One of the women said something like, 'It looks like we're going to be rained out. This never happened when True was here' and he replied 'True is closer to the controls now than she ever was and I'm not worried' and almost immediately the rain stopped and the sun came out."

In addition to chairing the Works Committee during her first term on Council, True served on all but two of the municipality's regular committees, was Chair of the Finance Committee and also of the Special Committees responsible for studying uses of Township lands and planning extensions to the Municipal Building.[6]

A formal portrait photo originally labelled 'True Davidson, CCF, York East.' ca. 1958. *Ashley & Crippen*

In 1960 she decided to run for Reeve at the urging of the president of the Ratepayer's Federation of East York "because it was felt that the previous mayor had acted unilaterally and that he had to be replaced. He said to me, you are the only one who can do it. I thought this was probably true because I was the best known. So I ran."[7] Her campaign literature stated that "I am offering myself for the Reeveship because I have been convinced by my own observations and by the arguments of my fellow citizens, including officers of almost all Ratepayer groups, that there must be a change."[8] Jack Christie was a member of a group opposed to the Rexleigh Apartments which Reeve Allen supported. He remembered that some of his group thought that Allen was in the pocket of the developers because he was close friends with some of the men who worked for it. "Feelings were so strong that one of the members of the residents' association followed Allen downtown after a Council meeting one time to the Lord Simcoe Hotel bar where he met representatives of the development company." He urged the ratepayers to "support True because he thought that she shared their philosophy and because he thought that she had the best chance of winning." He said that, when she was in hospital shortly before her death, she introduced him to someone "as the person who got me elected as Reeve the first time."

Charlotte Maher remembered True telling her that the campaign "was really hard-fought" and nasty because "scandal is unusual in municipal government in Metro. Councils may not have been smart but they have been pretty pure. But that was rough, rough going." Her printed material did not address the development controversy directly although they made a point of noting that she had "no customers or clients but you to please" and that she stood for "loyal adherence to Council decisions" and "high standards for redevelopment."[9] However, among her private papers, she kept the draft of a poem she obviously began to write at the time. No one remembers it being published or used in any form so it was probably written as a vent for her feelings during this, her first experience with a hard-fought election. The poem began by attacking Allen.

> I'm the democratic reeve of the Township of East York,
> I've been politically shifty since being brought here by the Stork
> I'm a two bit Tory follower, an ambitious party hack
> The ambition is position, with a shiny Cadillac.
>
> They all talk stuff and nonsense about honest public service,
> These mad crusading citizens don't even make me nervous,
> They preach of honest government, and leaving valleys green
> They don't know I'm protected by Granny Frost's very well-oiled machine

The poem then attacked her other opponents, saying of Royden Brigham that he was branding his opponents "With every kind of motive that's within my understanding"; of "Corporal" Norman Cheeseman that he was only in politics to find "openings for selling my insurance"; and calling Howard Chandler "a mobile tub of lard/He hasn't read the Plan at all, 'cause he finds brain work too hard."[10] It is doubtless fortunate that True kept this poem to herself.

The hottest issue of the campaign was the Reeve's development policy for the Township. True later wrote that "Jack Allen...was a brisk young landscape gardener, full of ambition and drive, for himself and his township. He seemed to see himself as a junior Fred Gardiner, developing East York as Fred was developing Metro, riding down all opposition with a jolly smile." He and his planning consultant, "an apartment architect named Sulio Venchiarutti...saw East York's future as one great apartment city, spreading from an arterial road in Taylor Creek valley, up both sides of the ravine." Allen pushed his plan through the Planning Committee, then Council turned it down, but couldn't muster the two-thirds vote to amend it. True noted that "Planning was at an impasse," and later wrote that "well do I remember the shocked glances which Mr. Blair, Mr. Brigham and I exchanged in the offices of Mr. Venchiarutti when we visited him soon after our election to see his plan. It showed a road through the valley (infamous in history as the Cosburn Avenue extension) with apartments lining both sides. In fact, there were apartments everywhere in the township."[11]

Willis Blair, Roy Brigham and she were "swept into council" in 1958 and "we got a new planning board. We got a planning commissioner of our own. We started on a plan which would represent the real desires of East York. And we fought a valiant, if largely unsuccessful, rear-guard defence of a freezing bylaw designed to prevent premature and undesirable development." She described them as being "as green as the grass and trees we were trying to save." They thought the ravines, at least, were safe because they would be protected by the Conservation Authority, but didn't know that Metro already had changed the route of the Bayview extension partly to "open up an undeveloped area" in East York's section of the Don Valley. "We saw the owners uprooting trees and changing contours, but Jack [Allen] assured us that he had spoken to them and that their operations had been necessitated by the road-building. After all, we had no suspicion that the reeve, disregarding our pledges to neighbours [in Leaside], had secured approvals from Metro, and that a reluctant building inspector had granted a permit for an apartment building, to be the first of a whole herd of "white elephants," on this choice bit of [valley land.]" The builders began construction immediately. "We advised them that the permit had been improperly issued. They put on extra shifts and worked under truck headlights. We advised them that they had not complied with our by-laws regarding unserviced properties, and that we would now refuse them services. And we did. And we stuck to it. That's why I call the famous "white elephant" on Bayview a monument to a council that wouldn't be coerced or cajoled." She said that it was "also a monument to Metro's greed for assessment" and that they had tried to mislead her when she asked about the Bayview extension and expropriation plans for the property. "It was a disillusioning experience....there's still a bad taste in my mouth when I remember."[12]

Although no one was ever charged in regards to these events, Doris Tucker well remembered the day when "the people from the Department of Municipal Affairs came up and interviewed the Building Inspector. He called and said, 'They want to talk to me about the passing of the permit for that building.' Jack Allen, you see, had sort of pushed that thing. He was a bit of a bully if he wanted to get his own way. He talked big and I guess he had to

"The Bayview Ghost" shortly before its demolition in 1981. It stood derelict for 13 years while various legal challenges to the halting of its construction made their way through the municipal and provincial governments. True described it as "a monument to a council that wouldn't be coerced or cajoled." *Courtesy Alan Redway*

prove himself down at Metro." The person from Municipal Affairs asked Doris to attend the interview, so "he came down...and asked questions and I said to him before [the Building Inspector] came in, 'this man's a very nervous man but he's one of the most honest men we have. Whatever he says will be the truth. Whatever he did was on the very best intentions.' So on that basis we started and he was there quite awhile. I'll never forget that. Poor old Freddy Wild [the Building Inspector.] I'll bet he was sick. You know when you're honest and you're trying to do a job and you know your job and other people are trying to push you around, why its terribly disheartening."

True defeated Allen handily, receiving 5,065 votes to his 3,458, largely as the result of the highest voter turnout (40%) in the township's history to that time. True told reporters that it had been a hard fight "but I couldn't be more touched by the confidence of the people in me." Allen did not appear at the township offices, never conceded the election and was obviously disappointed at the outcome. He was quoted as saying, "I find it's unpopular to do the right thing. I'm glad to get out. It will be a relief to get back to my family and job after so many years."[13]

True never forgot this struggle, asking years later "What are we to do with developers who destroy green belt land and then demand alternative zoning?" and noting that "In planning, it often seems municipalities have responsibility without power and nothing brings discredit to a law faster than inability to enforce it."[14]

The shell of the half-completed apartment building remained on the site until it was finally demolished in 1981, three years after True's death. East York's mayor at that time, Alan Redway, remembered it as "one of the happiest days of my term." He wrote of the long-drawn process of achieving demolition that:

Between 1960 and 1976, numerous attempts were made to solve the problem. Metro was asked but refused to expropriate the entire property. The owners requested but were refused permission to build three high-rise apartments....The building inspector declared the structure unsafe, but the owners repaired it...The borough tried to claim the property for unpaid taxes, but payment followed promptly after the claim was made....in 1976, the East York planning board began to develop a new official plan for the area [and]...the...lands were designated for either open space or for detached single family houses...the plan was sent to the Ontario minister of housing for his approval...[but]...sat on his desk from November 1977 until January 1979 when he received a request from the owners for a hearing at the OMB. The very next day the minister referred it to the board....In June 1979 [East York] obtained a special act of the Ontario Legislature permitting the municipality to enter the site, tear down the derelict structure and charge the costs of demolition to the owners ....Before the OMB, the owners presented their plan for 880 high rise and townhouse units which the borough, supported by the residents, countered with a plan for 66 single family detached homes....The board decided to approve 440 apartment and townhouse units for the site, and the borough appealed to the Ontario cabinet. In April [of 1981] the cabinet under the pressure of a provincial election campaign overturned the OMB decision and approved the borough's plan....[face-to-face discussions finally began with the owners and]...they proposed a peace treaty providing for demolition of the Ghost and construction of a single family detached subdivision. That sealed the White Elephant's fate, although the negotiations of the simple peace treaty took almost four months.... The White Elephant has been described as a monument to ratepayer action and vigilance. The new development will be a much more attractive monument.[15]

From this campaign she gained a reputation as a fighter for residential neighbourhoods, but Willis Blair remembered that she never expressed a clear definition of what made a development suitable. "She knew some of the old row houses in East York just had to be torn down...if she felt the developers were up-front about it and the community didn't object too much she'd allow it" although "she was big on making the developer set up a little parkette or something. There are a lot of those little parkettes around now [because of True.]" In effect, she wasn't opposed to development, she just wanted it to be orderly and acceptable to the community. As her honorary doctorate from York University stated, "she imparted her own intense concern with building and sustaining an environment congenial to the sustenance and growth of its every individual member."[16]

As always it is her poetry that best shows the sort of community that, emotionally, she most valued. She wrote the following poem for her 1964 Christmas card.

Between the factories of Toronto and Leaside,
North York's and Scarborough's looming towers,
East York has grown like an old-fashioned village
Where friendships flourish and children and flowers.

East York is full of neat little houses
On modest pieces of well-kept land
With neighbours to offer across the fences
A piece of their minds or a helping hand.[17]

Inaugural meeting of True's first term as Mayor of the Township of East York,
1961. *Courtesy Jack Christie*

There were other issues besides Planning for the new Reeve and
she took equal pride in them all. In the report published at the end
of her first year as Reeve she proudly announced that "East York
is running smoothly this year. We are all working together. That
doesn't mean that we always agree. But we are open and friendly
in our disagreements, and we know where we are with each
other." Among the accomplishments she credited to the Council
for the year were the establishment of cross-town transportation
almost to Dawes Road and that work was proceeding well on the
new Municipal Annex, Works Building and yards and the west-
end Community Centre, even though tax rates had risen less than
1/2 mill. Council was negotiating with property owners to allow
the municipality to undertake land reclamation on their ravine
slopes which had been ignored for several years and damaged by
dumping and erosion.

    She reported attending about forty meetings a month as a mem-
ber of 12 East York standing committees, two Metro Toronto committees and several special committees. Her proudest boast for the
year was that Metro was going to open its new island park on Dominion Day. She quoted one of the Metro Councillors as asking
"won't it cut into your East York celebration?" to which she replied,
"we aren't trying to monopolize patriotism. We'd like to see the
whole country en fete, not just the whole of Metro Toronto."[18]

True was already becoming the darling of the Toronto news-papers—someone who could always be counted on to provide a good quote or an interesting picture. She provided the perfect quote, "69,373 in Miss True's family" for an article about Metro politicians in which Colin Davies wrote of her schedule "In East York, Reeve True Davidson finds the hours long—but enjoys every moment. Also a 15-hour-day worker, she believes Sunday is a day of rest, keeping it free for anyone caring to drop into her Wood-mount Avenue home for a chat.…"I was never married so the township is my family," she says, pouring coffee for guests in front of a roaring log fire. In the living room Miss Davidson unwinds—but not for long. A portable telephone for plugging into whatever room Miss Davidson is occupying indicates municipal duties are only a phone call away."[19] Clara Thomas remembered that "she had terrific press. She was very photogenic" and that "she had an impeccable dignity so she could get away with an enormous amount of showing off—and she always did."

In 1962 True ran, successfully, for re-election. Her campaign literature noted that of the "seventeen campaign promises [from the 1960 campaign], fourteen have been fully or partially imple-mented. Only one, lower water rates, has been abandoned." It also noted that "you have heard True Davidson on radio and televi-sion. You have seen her sharing township activities from the British Empire Games Trials to a senior citizens's birthday" while at the same time playing an active role on the Metropolitan Coun-cil, Metro Planning Board and Metro Conservation Authority and that "in national and provincial municipal associations, she is the first East York reeve to play a major part in shaping policies to be urged on higher levels of government policies." East Yorkers, who had long suffered the mockery of larger municipalities and some newspapers who called the township "Least York", liked to see their reeve taking such a prominent role. They were proud that she had been asked to speak on "Municipal Ethics" to the Association of Ontario Mayors and Reeves and that her speech had to be reprinted several times afterwards. As the report on her first year in office concluded "The public image of East York has never been clearer or more colourful than under her leadership."[20]

True's speech on Municipal Ethics was one of the best pieces of writing she ever produced. Using humour, poetry and a wide variety of quotations she exhorted her fellow politicians to remember their oath of office where they had sworn to execute their offices "truly, faithfully and impartially." She spoke of how easily a corrupt government culture could develop as a result of lax decisions and told them to regard their oaths of office as positive, not negative things. "We do not fulfil them by refraining from conduct which might render us liable to prosecution. Too often our behaviour reminds me of the half-hearted service paid to the letter, but not the spirit, of the ten commandments:

> ...Thou shall not kill, but needst not strive
> Officiously, to keep alive.
> Thou shalt not steal—an empty feat
> When it's so lucrative to cheat

We're all nice respectable people. We don't want to break any laws. We just don't want to have them inconvenience us personally. Sure we don't kill or steal, but we ask the mayor...to fix parking tickets for us....We don't take bribes. Of course not. But where do we draw the line as to the presents and entertainment we will accept? Perhaps we seek popularity, yield to flattery, hunger for power, bask in public notice and acclaim, or are blinded by our own self-importance.... Some of us can be cowed by threats ...Some of us are influenced by racial or religious predispositions...All of these constitute conflict of interest which can never be reached by the long arm or probing finger of the law. Only we can spot them, and at that only if we scrutinize our own conduct as severely as we scrutinize the budget...Its chief executive can do much to set the cultural and moral tone of the community. A visitor...could learn much about the character of Toronto by watching Nathan Phillips in action...Insofar as our ideals are high, we lift our municipalities with us. If they are low, we drag them down." She led them through what she described as some of the "cheap, shoddy generalizations" that could lead a politician astray and urged her audience to develop "very fastidious noses" for the smell of dirty laundry. Having laid out the highest standards, she acknowledged that "all this is very high-sounding, and none of us is going to realize it, but you know the old saying: "Hitch your wagon to a star, and at least you won't trip over a dung-heap" and concluded by having them all recite the Athenian Oath:

We will never bring disgrace to our city by any act of dishonesty, or cowardice nor ever desert our comrades; we will fight for the ideals and sacred things of the city, both alone and with many; we will revere and obey the City Laws, and do our best to incite a like respect and reverence in others; we will strive unceasingly to quicken the public's sense of civic duty; and thus in all these ways we may transmit our city, greater, better and more beautiful than it was transmitted to us.[21]

Her colleagues generally agreed that True truly tried to live up to these standards herself. Jack Christie said "really all she wanted was to do what was good for East York" and that "she was going to do what was right regardless of the political compromises...she wasn't doing things now because it would help her at the next election. She had to think it was right." Clara Thomas felt that "as far as spending taxpayers money, she was totally ethical." Willis Blair remembered that "she was suspicious of anyone who earned over $100/day" and was uncomfortable with taking gifts of any sort. Doris Tucker remembered that if a developer "came in to see her, she's call me up. She'd say, 'Now, Doris, you stay right here because I want a witness. I don't want them to say I said something that I haven't.' East York was a good model municipality. It was well run." She added that "I must say about her, that East York was her pride. Everything that she did was for the betterment of East York. She was so proud of it." Gord Hazlett wrote that "I always voted for True because I thought she was a most honest politician."

She infuriated her colleagues regularly. As one of her obituaries said, "She fought with the aldermen, but the voters loved her."[22] Willis Blair remembered "I'd get mad as hell at her sometimes...but I learned a lot from her." True changed her vote on issues regularly, frustrating political opponents with her "casual ability to move unconcernedly from one side of the fence to the other, with occasional stops astraddle the fence in between." She admitted it but said "I simply have to weigh the pros and cons."[23] Doris Tucker remembered how the Council members "always bawled her out, because she'd go down to Metro and she'd ask the Council for their opinion on a certain thing that was coming up in Metro and then they'd all voice their opinion and she'd take it down with her and she'd say 'Well, I'll vote your way' and then when she got down there, well the circumstances changed so she would vote another way, and when she got back, believe you me, they would tell her." Doris remembered that True kept changing her mind about issues but "I always felt she'd have an attitude and then she'd hear something that was being done on the side and she wouldn't like it and then she would oppose it. Then that would be smoothed over and she would be back on track. There were a lot of things like that at Metro. She was fighting with them all the time or arguing with them. But it was always, I thought, in an effort to do the right thing."

Throughout her political career she struggled with well-hidden self-doubt about the value of her decisions. After her retirement she wrote, "I am glad I no longer have to struggle with...difficult decisions. No matter how one votes, one is likely to question oneself afterwards. Was I too much influenced by my personal interests? My sympathy? My prejudices? My desire to be re-elected? My trust in officials? My desire to see East York growing and recognized?"[24]

If True had a political weakness it arose from the fact she began to care too much about remaining Mayor. Charlotte Maher said that she "when she got the smell for it...getting people to do what she wanted, then it became an obsession." She believed deeply that she had finally achieved the position for which her entire career had trained her. As she told a reporter, when talking about how she had sought work without success earlier in her career, "They certainly wouldn't have advised me to take a job as Mayor of East York although that was obviously the job I was intended for by all my training and education."[25] This could lead her to become personally insulting to those who opposed her and her skill with words made her insults all the more painful and quotable by the media.

Near the end of her career True said that "when I first entered politics, I used to love to get into fights."[26] A reporter described her as as "...sharp and impatient, not unlike a combative rooster, red of countenance, feathers flying from her preposterous hats. 'Don't be addled, man!' she'd snap. 'Don't talk stupid.'" A former city councillor, Richard Horkins, remembered words "pouring out of her as hard as cannonballs. She always came right to the crunch point. No verbal sparring."[27] She was reported to have casually brushed aside rising Toronto alderman Tony O'Donohue as an "idiotic vulgarian." Royden Brigham, an East York lawyer who ran against True on several occasions, was the victim of some of her more classic comments. "True told one campaign audience that they could vote for her in complete confidence, because she vowed that when Brigham lost, she would personally make sure he did not go jobless. "Our solicitor, you see, needs a junior to assist him." She described Leslie Saunders, a former Toronto mayor who was later an East York alderman, as "bigoted, pigheaded, and in his attitude towards women, a throwback to the Stone Age."[28] Doris Tucker remembered her quarrelling with Leslie Saunders on several occasions. "Well, he was a little bit like her, you know. So he argued with her. The others they weren't used to standing up to someone who had such a good vocabulary—such a strong vocabulary. Even the bossiness, I think, they could have overcome that but I think it was the language...when she was arguing with you." After her 1969 election, she said of a competitor that "when I'm 71 in three years, I'll still be a better man than my opponent,"[29] and described two of her "bad boy aldermen, Howard Chandler and Norman Maughan, as the 'heavenly twins' with the implication that they are neither twins, nor heavenly."[30] John Dowling said of her that "her ego often matched [her] hats. Like most 'good talkers', she expected people to give way when she wanted to speak. Her precise, biting words could rasp the veneer from an official at 10 paces, sneak through a loophole, and suck the pomposity from a politician until he was reduced to a mewling baby. ...She was unique in a world where too many politicians have a cookie-cutter sameness."[31]

True frequently under-estimated the impact of her gibes and the exasperation and hard feelings that they could create. The Reeve of Long Branch, Tom Berry, was once goaded to explode, "Someone ought to spank True Davidson's bottom." Fred Gardiner once complained that she had "taken a yard of his hide. Miss Davidson shot back that he still had plenty of hide on his 230-pound frame." She didn't spare herself either. "Politicians," she once said, "suffered swollen egos, water on their lame brains, election fever and purse-string bursitis."[32]

Another reporter claimed that many of her aldermanic colleagues couldn't "stand the sight of her." One of them, Jack Irwin, was quoted as saying flatly, "none of us like her. Not a soul has a good word to say for her...behind her back....I call her False Davidson. To her face. At least I did until my wife made me stop because it was impolite." Yet even he said that "I think she rates with any of the mayors we have ever had in Metro. And as a politician, I think she is one of the top two or three in the whole of Canada. She is a very, very sharp individual. For sheer political astuteness, you can't beat her. I only wish you could." Veteran alderman Fred Beavis suffered from True's criticism on several occasions but, when asked what he thought about her, replied, "Let me give it to you this way. She's goes off on a tangent and lets go with a diatribe of words, which could upset you if you ever bothered to listen to them. But I personally pay taxes in East York, and dollar for dollar, we've had good administration from True Davidson."[33]

Clara Thomas remembered that True could be similarly difficult to handle in class, "for she had very very strong opinions and she did carry on about them, sometimes at too great length. However, the atmosphere she created was so dynamic and positive that we all thrived on it. One day I pounded the table and said, "True, why are you being so bitchy?" And she replied, "Because today you are all being so dull!" That smartened us all up—also gave us all a good laugh."[34] I wonder how many times she behaved as she did at Council because she thought the Councillors were "all being so dull?"

Most of her famous insults just made East Yorkers laugh, but she could go too far. Jack Christie remembered one time. "That was the worst I ever saw her. At a meeting in the school she called him [Leslie Saunders] bigoted, biased, etc....She believed it and thought it would get her votes. Instead she was booed. Not by the whole audience but by quite a few. Only time I ever saw her booed. They had never seen her behave that way and they didn't like it." True was aware of the dangers inherent in this aspect of her character, but couldn't seem to always control it. As a reminder, she kept a poem which reminded her, "Had fate assigned your/dreadful fault to me/ What charming little foibles/They would be!"[35]

8

METRO COUNCIL AND THE
FIGHT AGAINST AMALGAMATION
1962–1966

When True was first elected as Reeve she vowed not to "try to make a splash" on Metro Council, but said she would "sit and learn and do the best I can."[1] Circumstances—and her own personality—soon made this resolution impossible. William Kilbourn, a historian and respected Toronto councillor, described her as "a thorn in the flesh of the smooth men at Metro." Dick Beddoes wrote that "she was an independent...rarely succumbing to blandishments in exchange for her vote. Metro affairs frequently revolve around the boroughs versus the city, the Metro chairmen generally certain of a majority by seducing susceptible borough politicians. Miss Davidson would have none of it."[2] She told the Association of Mayors and Reeves of Ontario that she had been told by a distinguished Metro politician that "you've got to go along to get along," but that she didn't believe it. "Anything got by going along with what we don't believe in does something so bad to us that it outweighs any good it might seem to bring...to the municipalities we are sworn to serve. I do not believe the township of East York would want anything I got for it by these means. Certainly they wouldn't want me if they thought I'd done such a thing."[3]

As soon as True arrived on Metro Council she began to scrap with its Chairman. Chairman Frederick Gardiner was famous for his ability to overwhelm his opponents and to dominate the proceedings. True wrote of him that, "Personally I was very fond of

Mr. Gardiner. Unlike some of the women who served on Metro Council, I was never alarmed by his voice or language or hectoring manner. I had come from the world of business, not from the protection of a home, and I had met tougher characters than Fred Gardiner in my day." She described him as a bulldozer, noting that "when I call him a bulldozer, I am not being critical. A bulldozer knocks things about a bit, but not wantonly. There is a purpose, and usually the purpose is to prepare for construction."[4]

Gardiner was succeeded by Albert Campbell, whom some described as "a maundering chairman, inclined to regard other councillors as grade one dunces ruled by himself as schoolmaster." Kilbourn recalled that "True would scoff down to Campbell. She'd be scornful. 'Speak up!' she'd say. 'Don't mutter.'"[5] Joan Moore remembered meeting True "around 1957 on the Yonge Street subway and by this time she was on Metro Council. She told me how much it bothered her when members talked and yelled when she was talking."[6]

While True became known to the rest of Metro "as a colorful character from the pocket borough" the people of East York "identified her as their voice on Metro Council."[7] *The Toronto Star* described her as dauntless, "a forceful voice in Metro Toronto politics, out-spoken, aggressive, exasperating to her colleagues and winner of many a council debate as often by quick wit as pure logic."[8] Jack Christie said that while he didn't have much to do with Metro Council, he felt that "she was effective and she couldn't have gotten all she did for East York there if she hadn't been capable or had alienated the members of Metro Council or its bureaucracy." *The Toronto Star* wrote of her that "despite her age...she is one of the keenest participants on the moribund Metro Council."[9]

True became famous what Kilbourn called "her crazy stands." She told the Metro Executive Committee that Toronto's cab drivers "look like thugs" and that they frightened her so much that at times she took "a good clutch on my purse" when got into a cab.[10] She argued that Metro should begin limiting its population growth by cutting back on services such as the provision of water and sewerage facilities.[11] She exclaimed that she was "tired of Serbs and Estonians and Croats bringing their Old World feuds here" when Councillor William Boytchuk sought to have Metro pay the legal expenses of the Ukrainian-Canadian Committee for the judicial inquiry called to investigate the demonstrations during Soviet Premier Alexei Kosygin's visit to Toronto in 1970.[12] She attacked the province for "pussyfooting, temporizing and vacillating" on matters vital to Metro, and causing the loss of thousands of jobs.[13] She branded drinking drivers as "motor criminals" in her support for compulsory breath tests.[14]

She was cool to the proposal to build a subway line along Eglinton Avenue, saying, "Sure, it would be good for East York and other boroughs, but for Metro as a whole, it wouldn't help. The Eglinton line wouldn't do anything at all for the CNE, or the planned Metro Centre on the waterfront, or anyone in the southeast areas." She added that the Eglinton route would still empty into the Yonge Street transit line, causing overflow.[15]

Alan Redway remembers when True decided that the new municipality needed a new chain of office for its Mayor and approached all the community's service clubs for a contribution. He was then president of the Leaside Lions Club and originally declined "but True was never one to take no for an answer and she kept calling and pushing and eventually we found the money somehow" *Courtesy Emily Smith*

Despite her previous career in the C.C.F., she became a strong opponent against the provision of expensive social services to the unemployed. As usual she would do anything to help an individual in need but resisted assistance to disadvantaged groups. She voted against giving free dental care to people on welfare because, she said, "I come from East York which is a working class community where many of the workers were earning little or less than the people on welfare. And they couldn't look after their own teeth or their children's teeth. So I couldn't vote to take their taxes to pay for dental care for children on welfare. I would vote for it if it were extended to cover everyone under a certain income level."[16] She used the same argument when opposing reduced fares for seniors on the TTC saying that seniors as a group were no more deserving than poor families.

Despite her stands, many of her opponents continued to respect, and even love, her. June Callwood remembered "I even loved her for voting to have the city sue me for failure to pay the rent on Digger House. In my defense, we stopped paying the rent not only because we had no money but because the city was being a negligent landlord in order to force us to leave—wiring was dangerous, for instance. True said she would rather scrub floors than owe anyone money. I never held that against her. I felt much the same."[17]

True claimed that the Canadian Council on Social Development was controlled by radicals and resigned from the board of directors of the Social Planning Council of Metropolitan Toronto because she believed the council was "being taken over by anarchistic welfare recipients and their supporters." She argued, paternalistically, that the recipients wouldn't be able to be objective. "I just want it [social assistance] to be given intelligently. The more you give them the more they feel entitled to and the more they demand. Instead they should be taught to help themselves."[18] She wrote that "one of the most idiotic suggestions I've ever heard was the idea that over half of the Canadian Welfare Council should be made up of people on public assistance. It's like saying that over half of any medical clinic should be made up of patients."[19]

Her controversial statements were received much like her personal attacks. While most accepted them as part of her colourful character and respected her for speaking her mind, they tended to reinforce the image of her among her opponents as a "loose cannon"—albeit a highly intelligent one.

She was strongly opposed to the introduction of political parties into the municipal system, blaming it for the "carrying on at the Metro level."[20] She told the Association of Mayors and Reeves that "when we meet in council we do not meet as a government and an opposition, with predetermined positions. We all work together for the common good, and every member has a right to hold his independent views and make his independent contribution. Let us never forget that the party system was devised by one of the most corrupt prime ministers Britain ever had. It was devised simply and solely for the purpose of keeping himself and his friends in office. I do not think it has changed very much since Walpole's day, and I do not think that any opposition can prevent a government from graft and corruption if enough people profit by it or think it can't be bucked."[21]

Fire Department photograph of True and Beth Nealson riding in the open car at the front of the Dominion Day Parade.

One of the major issues to face the Metropolitan Toronto Council during her terms was that of the proposed Spadina Expressway. City politicians, including William Kilbourn, Colin Vaughan, Anne Johnston and John Sewell, fought feverishly to stop its construction. True changed her vote on the issue repeatedly, sympathizing with the desire of the residents to save their neighbourhoods from demolition and with their arguments against the "car culture" which its construction supported, but desiring the jobs and business growth which the plan promised to produce. She was also a strong believer in maintaining the authority of municipalities, so, once the plan had been approved by Metro Council and had passed the Ontario Municipal Board, she felt it wrong for the provincial government to interfere. She raged against the cabinet decision that cancelled its construction as "stupidity, pig-headedness and arrogance," said that it had thrown Metro politics into confusion and warned that its rejection "endangered" Metro's authority.[22] However, despite her ever-changing opinions, and general opposition to his cause, William Kilbourn remembered that "True was one of the few borough politicans we could turn to. She'd take crazy stands, but she'd raise stuff in Metro transportation meetings that was vital to us."[23]

The greatest battle in which she engaged during her first two terms as Reeve was waged against the Goldenberg Commission's plans for amalgamation. Their preliminary recommendation that East York be eliminated as a separate township within Metro caused her to fight back "with tigerish tenacity.[24]

Willis Blair remembered that "Goldenberg had a lot of respect for True," and Doris Tucker said that "True really fought because she really thought East York was going to be swallowed up." Doris remembered when True had all the senior township staff go over to talk to Carl Goldenberg one Saturday morning. "She bullied him into meeting us. And we all had to talk about what we did in East York and give him a good picture of East York so he would know that we were a good viable municipality and as she said, "100,000 population isn't to be sneezed at. That's a better type of population than a great big one and if they put us in with some of the others it wouldn't be nearly as well run." And maybe it did influence him because he recommended that we remain East York."

East York's brief to the Commission used every possible argument against the absorption of East York and included a fascinating series of quotations supplied, without doubt, by True from her varied readings and experiences. Urging that changes only occur after careful thought and planning, she mocked "the absurd system of representation on the Metropolitan Toronto Council" and quoted a "distinguished politician" as having told her that it had been devised out of "Expediency, my dear girl, just expediency." She urged the Commission to decide the sort of municipal government they really wanted before making changes, and quoted the Cheshire cat who, when asked by Alice in Wonderland, "what way ought I to go from here?", responded "That depends a good deal on where you want to go to."

As part of the defence for the preservation of East York as a small community, she quoted Elwyn Brooks White, "It is easier

for a man to be loyal to his club than to his planet: the by-laws are
shorter and he is personally acquainted with the other members."
She cited Jane Jacobs, urging that the municipality needed to remain small so that "a district [could be] big and powerful enough
to fight City Hall."

Official photograph of the 1963 Metropolitan Toronto Council. True is shown
third from the right in the front row. *Courtesy the Todmorden Mills Heritage
Museum and Arts Centre*

Refuting claims that a larger municipality would be more efficient in its urban planning she quoted Ernest van den Haag's report. "City planning'...seems to be largely in the hands of people
who hate cities and have no understanding whatever of what
makes cities more than aggregates of building and traffic lanes."
The brief also included pages of statistical comparisons showing
that East York's assessment was growing and healthy and that its
per capital assessment had gone up less than in many other Metro
municipalities.

In addition, True submitted a "personal summary" to the
Commission in which she listed some of the personal beliefs about
she said formed the "sub-conscious computer" which sorted information in the back of her brain. These included statements
such as: "Individual differences and individual integrity are too
valuable to be merged in...the regimented stereotype; the big city,
the big machine;" "The...ability...of citizens to work for what

they want is more important than the exact amounts...which result;" "There are minimum and maximum sizes for efficient and
well co-ordinated operation in a committee, a council and a municipality—indeed in any social or political unit;" and finally her
assertion that "It is as bad for a man to deprive him of a sense of
his own significance as to deprive him of food. Because he is gre-
garious, he can only achieve this sense of significance if he feels
himself part of a community which is doing things together." She
affirmed that, for all its limitations, East York had for her personally, after all her experiences living in many communities "as the
daughter of an itinerant Methodist clergyman and in a succession
of jobs," come "nearest to providing its citizens adequately with
the needs...above."

She assured the commission that "East York has within it a
rare vitality...its people wish to survive as a group. This is not because of any especially favourable financial position, for the township enjoys none. It has the lowest per capita population in Metro.
But for several years it has been buying equipment and paying for
projects out of current income when other and richer communities
have been debenturing for them. ...East York is small enough to
know what services and amenities its people want and need, and
large enough to supply them....More than 700 people are engaged
in some sort of voluntary work with or for the township and there
is a remarkable sense of fellowship...We have pioneered in many
fields of education and recreation. There is a tremendous community pride, which gives residents a sense of belonging, of security
and of significance."

She concluded with a story told her by an investigator for the
Metro Housing Authority which she felt summed up the feeling of
East Yorkers for their township. "The room was small and rather
untidy for the mother was young and there were three babies. She
was almost crying as she apologized, and said she must somehow
get into decent housing. 'I'm not accustomed to living like this,'
she said. 'I was brought up in East York.' To her it was something
to live up to and work for. East York is that to all of us."[25]

She lobbied vigorously in the newspapers and at all levels of
the provincial government, right up to and including the Premier.
Whether it was True who influenced Goldenberg's decision or not
will never be known for certain, but his final report recommended
merging East York with its smaller neighbour, Leaside, rather

than that both be eliminated. The Commission's recommendation was approved and work began on the logistics of the merger.

Leaside had fought fully as hard to preserve its autonomy and many of its residents were angered by the decision to merge it with East York. The town benefited from a strong industrial tax base and Leaside residents enjoyed the resultant services and low residential taxes and feared higher taxes and lower services as "their" revenues were "sucked up" by East York. Doris Tucker felt that some Leaside residents believed that being part of East York would lower their social status. "A lot of them had lived in East York and when they got a bit more money they moved up to Leaside. They felt they were a little better off. We were the south side of the tracks and they were the north side of the tracks."

Doris remembers that it took quite "a little time for everyone to adjust" to the new situation. The two Councils met and discussed how things were to work and True "spoke to the staff and said it would be nice if we could absorb those people up there. So for a whole year, I never took on staff. I needed help but I think about 3 people left so we were able to take everybody [from the

Mayor Beth Nealson with the Leaside Council, ca. 1966. *Courtesy the Todmorden Mills Heritage Museum and Arts Centre.*

Leaside Clerks Department.]" "I was appointed Municipal Clerk
and the late Fred Cook, the former clerk of Leaside, was named
Deputy Clerk. As a matter of fact the staffs of both municipalities
were entirely integrated and all had to be appointed as members of
the newly formed borough staff."[26]

The 1966 election campaign for the new Borough did little to
improve relations. True Davidson was certainly not the sort of
politician to which Leasiders were accustomed! Her main competitors were Royden Brigham and the former Leaside Mayor,
Beth Nealson, and the campaign was described by one Toronto
newspaper as a "bombastic, free-wheeling affair." With complete
confidence in herself, True sent "an open letter to the people of
Leaside" which she designed to present her "credentials where I
am less well known."[27] This sort of dignified campaigning didn't
last long. True was soon quoted as having said, "I'm no wishy-
washy, sissy little sweetheart" with the implication that Beth
Nealson was, and as calling Brigham, "a defenseless little creature." He reportedly said that he has claws, but vowed "to remain
a gentleman forever."[28] True told a ratepayer's group that "if you
want someone beautiful and elegant, or glamorous, I'm not
that."[29] Voter interviews from the time overwhelmingly disap-
proved of these personality clashes with comments like "The hurl-
ing of abuse and insults during campaigns is most degrading" and
Candidates can clash by their fiery personality, but it should not
descend to unmannerly abuse and insults. This is not businesslike,
and it really insults the voter." One voter, however, acknowledged
that "it does put excitement into the meetings. After all, candidates are in there fighting to win...and they can't always be calm
and polite."[30]

True finished the campaign in hospital recovering from a heart
attack, but won an easy victory at the polls. Jack Christie remembered that she was pleased to have been retained as Mayor "not
really exultant though—just satisfied," and that she just "seemed
to regard as another challenge" the problem of how to handle the
bad feelings that resulted from the merger. He said that "she
wanted to keep Leaside as much like it was as possible. She made
no attempt to absorb it—just to add it on."

Although True had won the election, she remained opposed
to future amalgamations, stating firmly that she was "against
total amalgamation of the city and the five boroughs because

politicians can't get close enough to the people in such a system."[31] Years later, in her column for the *Toronto Sun*, she praised Hazel McCallion for resisting the amalgamation of Streetsville into South Peel, writing: "Go to it, Hazel! However parochial your aims, if you can substitute orderly, reasonable growth for the destruction of one community, all the communities in Ontario will call you blessed."[32]

9

A WOMAN IN POLITICS

"*S*ir, a woman preaching is like a dog walking on his hinder legs. It is not done well; but you are surprised to see it done at all,"[1] This quotation, which True attributed to Samuel Johnson, was one of her favourites when describing how she and other women were viewed when they began to break into business and politics.

Her entire career was a list of feminine firsts. She was among the small, select group of female M.A. students to graduate from Victoria College; she was the first woman's sales representative in Canadian publishing when she worked at J.M. Dent & Sons in the 1920s; she worked as chief of staff for Perkins Bull where she supervised a staff of 20-70 men and women; she was the first woman to serve as Chairman of the East York Board of Education; and the first female Reeve of East York. Her opinions on women's issues were continually solicited—and offered.

Her opinions on women's rights were as individual as on all the others she expressed during her career and were as likely to infuriate feminists as to inspire them. She acknowledged that she had to struggle harder than any man to achieve her position simply because she was a woman. Emily Smith remembered her saying that "They didn't want to be upped by a woman. 'This is the man's level, now you just stay a little below.'"

She wrote of her experiences on the Canadian National Exhibition Board that "All of the men on [it] would be described by the women's liberation group in language unsuitable for print, and yet with which I cannot but largely agree." She remembered a time when the women on the Board were objecting to "Women's Day" as being a "patronizing concession...putting them on a level with children, who also required special concessions and attractions. Finally, in desperation, I said, "then why not have a men's day ?"

Oakah [Jones] looked at me with that radiant smile, and made the retort of his CNE career: "But True," he said kindly, "every day is men's day."[2] A voter opinion survey conducted during the 1966 election quoted an elector who told her, "Women should not enter politics. Personalities should not enter issues. Elections should be based solely on issues."[3]

Jim Lister, who used to serve as her chauffeur on occasion, remembered that "being a woman in a mostly male profession, many times she was under a great deal of pressure."[4]

True wearing one of her trademark hats.
Courtesy Emily Smith

She told an audience once that all politicians were objects of some curiosity and that women politicians were regarded as even stranger. "Some people who show an interest in politicians act as if they were visiting the zoo: How do we survive the hostile climate, what do they feed us...how do women survive?"[5]

She told a female reporter that "It's much more difficult for women in politics because men don't naturally accept the leadership of females" and that "the men that I defeat think I'm re-elected just because I'm popular but the people who re-elect me must have some trust in my ability. However, she said there were only two women on the 33-member Toronto Metro Council despite the fact that there are so many capable women in that city." She claimed that she felt no bitterness about the position of women but said that "organizations like the Women's Liberation Movement are understandable because women are in an inferior position."[6]

She explored the subject of what made a "womanly woman" at some depth in her book, *The Golden Strings*. In one poem she wrote:

I am a person
Emily Murphy and Nellie McClung and Irene Parlby proved it...

They proved it with Louise McKinney and Henrietta Muir Edwards...

But not one of those five magnificent women was ever appointed to
the Senate
Men don't like being proved wrong
Especially by women.

The same poem went on to talk of how Prime Minister Louis St.
Laurent had failed to appoint Agnes Macphail to the Senate even
though opinion polls showed that a majority of Canadians wanted
him to.

After all she had been a CCFer
And she wasn't a womanly woman either,
Not by his standards.
She didn't know her place.

What is the place of a woman?
A woman lives to love and suffer and understand,
To suffer pain and injustice without making men uncomfortable,
To understand the needs of her country and community and people
And put them above her own desires and needs.

It is a woman's place to be slapped down again and again
For presenting the needs of people to those who could help,
And to present them again in another way,
And again,
Firmly, gently, without arrogance or bitterness,
Until at last the needs are recognized everywhere
And some man is praised for the brilliant discovery.[7]

True soon developed a thick public skin, but she could still be
hurt by male mockery. Among her papers is a newspaper photograph of her, dressed in shorts, with her stockings rolled down,
helping to pull garbage out of the Don River. Above it she wrote a
note. "They were making jokes and snide remarks, concerning

and relating to this picture, and [Vernon] Page made the gang laugh when he said, "it's too bad she wasn't wearing "hot pants." [Arthur] Meen enjoyed the goings-on and himself threw in a few darts."[8] Dalton Morrison recalled that "just under the crust was a super-sensitive person who when alone did much retrospective soul-searching with concomitant pain and anguish."[9]

Many admired her refusal to be daunted by being the only woman in the all-male preserves of the municipal councils of her day. *The Toronto Star*, asserted that "She proved it was no handicap being a female in politics even in the days when political parties weren't beating the bushes looking for women candidates. She bears emulating by any woman with political ambitions."[10] She enjoyed needling men over their endless debates. "Men are talkers, women are doers," she would claim. It was said that her "sharp, hawk-like features made her perfect for the role of henpecking hapless male councillors."[11]

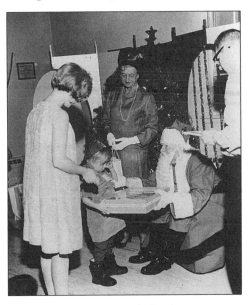

The Mayor, centre, attends fire department Christmas party. *Courtesy East York Fire Department)*

Her features were not her only striking attribute. Her entire appearance created a powerful presence. She was unusually tall and angular and her face was very striking and memorable—especially her eyes. She always looked like she needed sleep—her eyes were peculiarly pale and surrounded by deep bags—but they expressed her moods clearly and could stare down the strongest opponent. Her height was accentuated by the erectness of her posture and she had an unusual, uncomfortable-looking manner of walking that made her easily identifiable in a crowd—even if she wasn't wearing a hat.

She was quoted as saying that "men anywhere aren't too genuine in what they promise a woman,"[12] and wrote about how men built up their egos by making fun of women and patronizing and petting them, concluding that "You can't have a good partnership without mutual respect, and you can't have mutual respect without some recognition of your strengths and weaknesses."[13] In her newspaper column she wrote about how people make selfish decisions that help others and asked what we should say "of the man

who reduces his wife from the status of a partner to that of a charming but brainless pet, or a self-sacrificing but lifeless drudge? What of the wife who exploits her husband (and there are plenty of those too)?"[14]

Ian Urquhart wrote in 1972, that "Miss Davidson has built her political career not on an intricate structure of alliances but on personal charisma. If she steps down rather than seek re-election this December, Metro will not only lose one of its most independent politicians, but a feminist shrine."[15]

True wearing chain of office and floppy black hat. *Ashley and Crippen*

True told the Hamilton Women's Canadian Club that Canada is "a woman's country. It was from the beginning. This country was built on patience, fortitude and faith. Those are women's qualities. Women are creators and preservers. Men are adventurers."[16]

She developed her own means of working within the constraints of her world, many of which would generate some winces among women today. Jeanne Hughes remembered once time when the board of the Metropolitan Toronto and Region Conservation Authority met in the restored Town Hall at Black Creek Pioneer Village where she worked. "The men were all at one end of the

Her Worship arrives to inspect the East York Fire Department. *Courtesy East York Fire Department*

table talking seriously about something like the budget and True and two other—pretty high-powered women who were on the board—were at the other end urging each other to eat more of the cookies we'd put out for them and True was acting all girlish and saying "I really shouldn't" and they were saying she didn't have to worry and I was embarrassed to see these women behaving this way."[17] True sometimes used this "feminine act" deliberately. Other times it was selected for her, as in the newspaper account of her first Council win which noted that, at the victory party, she was busy making mayonnaise for more sandwiches.

In 1967, she was quoted as explaining that "her political success stemmed from a knack for handling male antagonism. Females in politics should avoid being too forward for fear that men should regard them as monsters invading their club. If I am very enthusiastic about an issue," she confided, "I make sure someone else suggests supporting it."[18] She told another group that she always wore dark colours so as not to antagonize the men on Council. She used a picture of herself knitting on her election flyer for at least two campaigns, with the slogan, "True Davidson can knit together the whole community."[19] After declaring that the Women's Liberation Movement had reason for its anger, she qualified the statement by saying that "But I think a lot of women would rather help a strong man than themselves and I would have done the same if there had been one around."[20]

She congratulated Margaret Campbell on being nominated to run for the provincial Liberals in the St. George riding saying that this wasn't "because you're a woman, though goodness knows we've also got more than enough men there already. It wouldn't make any difference what sex you were if you belonged to the theory-dominated, opposed-to-everything NDP or the success-oriented, patronage-based Conservatives. But being a Liberal, you're allowed some latitude to think for yourself, and being a woman—and a wife and mother—you bring to your thinking a sensitivity, an awareness of individual needs, that is rare among men...Yours is a...brisk common sense, backed by a gut feeling for the people."[21]

True circa 1968. *Courtesy Emily Smith*

Jack Christie remembered that "being a woman was no advantage or disadvantage to her. She was just True Davidson. One of the few people who was just automatically accepted. She had such a personality. She could put it on too. She could use her personality and intelligence to leave people awestruck or she could use it the other way also. If it looked like she was losing a debate she'd say, "Well, if that's the way you all feel about it, I guess that's how it will have to be. After all, what do I know. I'm just the daughter of a poor country minister." That way, she avoided the appearance of a defeat and took away the victory."

Doris Tucker also remembered this technique. "She could get her way with men. I can remember her arguing with Les Saunders one night…and saying,…after they had been arguing for about an hour. "Well, all you men have wives that you can go home to and tell your troubles to and I don't have a husband to go home to. I'm just a poor single woman," she said. And poor Les Saunders said, "Oh, I know True. It's alright. We forgive you," or something like that and they changed their minds and stopped arguing with her. And I thought, "My gosh, can't she get around them."

She used her reputation as "caustic lady"[22] to persuade men to do what she wanted, and claimed that "The men sometimes think I lose my temper, but this is a technique when I think they are not listening to me. I get mad at them and fly off, but this is [as] different from losing your temper as winter is from sunshine. That is why men have ulcers more than women because they have been taught that they must not go into tantrums, and they must not cry. Women have more durability than men because they do have an outlet for their feelings. This is one of the difficulties for women in business or public life. You have to control yourself. You musn't let yourself go. Unless you do it for effect."[23]

Like many who have succeeded despite the discrimination they had to face, True had little sympathy or understanding for many of the "women's issues" of her day. She had no sympathy for what she viewed as an admission of weakness—the idea that women needed special concessions to succeed. If she could succeed, so could any one woman with sufficient energy and drive! Dalton Morrison recalled that when she became the first woman to chair the East York Board of Education and again to chair the finance committee of the Metropolitan Toronto School Board, she "challenged women teachers to stop complaining, to qualify, and to apply for posts of responsibility."[24]

True infuriated many when she wrote, "Women, who should be custodians of the values of the race, are fussing around about their rights, insisting on being called Ms. and chairperson as if a change in title made you more or less than you were originally. Insisting on abortions because they are too lazy and shiftless to practise birth control or abstinence."[25] Her neighbour, Gord Hazlett, recalled that "Of course, her name was Miss True Davidson." Clara Thomas remembered that True "was very language conscious. She loved language and, of course, she was very King James conscious, like all of her generation and would always consider that the height of the English language."

On another occasion, True told a conference of women seeking political office that being liberated was not enough reason to run for politics. She recalled that she ran for school trustee because of her belief in the need for kindergartens in the schools and said that people who did not have solid issues should stay out of politics. "Mrs. Something-or-other shouldn't be running for anything."[26] She applied the same standard to men however, urging her "friends to choose their governments wisely. To choose representatives who follow their consciences to their own hurt. Who try to give more than they get. Who try to see all sides of a question before making a decision on it. Who try to enlarge our minds, not our public monuments. Who don't talk about things but do them. My grandmother used to say that a lot of people were all froth and no cider. We know which we are ourselves, and they say we always get the government we deserve."[27]

When she encountered a woman whom she felt met these high standards she supported them, even if it meant crossing party lines. June Callwood remembered seeing "her turn up at a fundraiser for Flora MacDonald's leadership of the Tories campaign. The party was called Fifty for Flora and was held in the McGill Club. Isabel Bassett and I were hosts and we got all-party support for Flora. The most striking woman in the room was True."[28]

In 1967, she told *The Toronto Star* that a woman in public life "should be able to fight vigorously and afterwards be able to go out for a drink with her opponents without any rancor about earlier clashes. Women are too easily distracted. They don't keep their eyes on a single goal. There's no reason women should not be as successful as men in politics."[29]

However, as long as they had a cause to support, True encouraged participation by the women in East York in politics. Many of her political supporters and campaign workers were drawn from the many womens' groups to which she belonged, and when she had a new cause it was not uncommon to see her organize a group of women as its first supporters.[30]

Dick Beddoes wrote of her that "Miss Davidson was a feminist far in advance of Uppity Women Unite, a long-time advocate of petticoat power. In 1975, International Women's Year, she chided the liberationists-come-lately. "Call me Miss Davidson," she told me. "The libbers' Ms is so coy."[31] To many feminists, these statements by her were virtual treason. Charlotte Maher said that True "wasn't a strong supporter of feminism, in part because everyone would be like her. She liked being the only woman."

June Callwood probably defined her value best when she wrote that "in many ways she was a role model for women without knowing it: she was just being herself, crusty and combative, at a time when few women dared to be either."[32]

Despite later health concerns, True's spirit of doing predominated. *Courtesy Emily Smith*

At the beginning of her political career, True had been laughed at because of the way she dressed. She couldn't affort to dress well then, but once she had a steady income—and some fashion advice—she turned her wardrobe, and especially her hats, into a political weapon, guaranteed to ensure her coverage and usually a photograph in the newspaper. It was a rare story about True that didn't include some mention of her outfit. Article after article included phrases like, "Wearing a green tulle hat, the only lady top executive of a Metro borough charmed a dinner meeting of the Junior Board of Trade,"[33] and "She looked fit election night, sporting a two-piece emerald green dress, matching shoes and purse, a white mink jacket and pulled-down hat."[34]

She told a reporter that "her intention isn't…to be a trend settler. "But I feel I owe to my ratepayers to be well dressed just as much as I owe them the responsibility of speaking clearly, using good English and representing them properly and with dignity." The reporter noted that she also dieted rigidly to main her 145-pound average and that she changed gloves at least twice during a reception. "It's not that people have dirty hands but after shaking 300 of them, you just have to change gloves."[35]

Doris Tucker remembered that "True had a hundred hats. After she was on Council she could buy some clothes for herself. Every time they had some nice things at Simpsons, you know, The Room, the lady down there would call her and down she'd go. And so she had an outfit and the shoes and the gloves and the hat to go with that outfit and a room where they were all kept in order." True told a group at Mohawk College that she began to wear a hat because her hair was wispy. Her hair was another of her unique features, grey and unusually fine and silky. One of Clara Thomas' students asked True when she began to collect hats and was told, "I used to be on many committees where I was the only woman. And I found out that if I had a new hat on, the men all paid so much attention to it that they often weren't aware of the political moves I was making during the meeting. My hats have been very much to my advantage. And then, of course, the press loved them, and people began to give me hats in thanks for speaking engagements."[36] Clara also recalled that True "loved to splurge on jewellery and clothes. She bought amazingly expensive clothes, very high fashion. She knew what was to her advantage. Well-dressed at all times. She loved it." Clara also wrote of a gold and garnet pin and earrings set which she purchased from True's estate, which she has since passed on to "Naomi Black, who was a pioneer in women's causes at York, and I know that she in her turn will pass on the True Davidson jewellery to some other outstanding woman."[37] Charlotte Maher believes that "True was not in the slightest vain. It was a political game, that hat business. Her selection of clothes was mechanistic, everything by colour. It wasn't a matter of taste. It just served a purpose." The citation for her honorary degree from York University put it best. "In her public life she has always had a chieftain's presence—and on the head of True Davidson, alone among Canadian women of her time, a lady's hat became a political weapon, charming, formidable and renowned."[38]

10

MAYOR OF EAST YORK

1967–1969

*F*aced with the challenge of merging two proud municipalities into one, True used the public celebrations associated with Canada's Centennial to create opportunities for individuals and groups from each area to work together. Doris Tucker remembered how many activities were planned to celebrate Canada's Centennial year and "also the birth of a new municipality... We started off with a New Year's Eve service in the Council Chambers and later in the month a Centennial Ball was held...at the Inn on the Park. Everyone attending was encouraged to wear period costumes. Many did, both men and women. It was a beautiful sight to see the women in lovely silk and satin bouffant gowns swirling around the dance floor on the arms of the men in their elegant period costumes. Of course, the belle of the ball was True Davidson, in a gorgeous rose pink gown, trimmed with a grecian key design in purple around the bouffant skirt. ...True wore the same gown throughout the year at many other Centennial celebrations."[1]

East York's largest celebration during that Centennial year was the official opening of the Todmorden Mills Museum on Pottery Road in the Don Valley. It is likely that Charles Sauriol was responsible for getting True interested in this site. He had written about its history on several occasions in his newsletter, *The Cardinal*, during the early 1960s as part of his campaign to educate people about the environmental and historical significance of the Don Valley. If so, True proved to be one of his most productive converts—throwing all of her extraordinary energy, enthusiasm and position into the preservation of the remaining historic structures on the site and, later, into the restoration of the valley's seriously damaged environment. I have heard suggestions, however, that the relationship between True and Sauriol soon became strained as the project advanced. Both had very strong, dominant personalities and viewpoints and Sauriol soon had to stand aside from the project and let True take centre stage.

In 1967, the Todmorden site consisted of four of the original structures of the old mill village of Todmorden: a frame house attributed to Parshall Terry, a mud-brick and board-and-batten house attributed to William Helliwell, the Taylor/Davies paper mill and the shell of part of the Helliwell Brewery. The train station was moved to the site several years later.

Historically, the village had begun in 1793 when Lieutenant-Governor John Graves Simcoe granted a lot on the river to Aaron and Isaiah Skinner on the understanding that they would build a saw-mill on the site at their own expense. This was Toronto's (then the Town of York's) second saw-mill; an urgently needed facility for the building supplies necessary for Simcoe's planned new capital. This mill opened in 1795 and was so successful that Simcoe rewarded the Skinners with the right to erect York's first grist mill on the site the following year. In 1797 one of the town's first roads was cut along the edge of valley rim to reach the mills. Then called, the Don Mills Road it followed essentially the same route as modern-day Broadview Avenue.

Over the century, a village grew up around the mill-sites and new industries moved to the site. In 1820, the Helliwell family purchased half of the property and constructed a brewery. John Eastwood and Colin Skinner, Isaiah's son, constructed a paper mill on the other half of the property—the second one in the province. These industries prospered until the middle of the 19th century. The brewery was destroyed by fire in 1849 and the Helliwell property was eventually sold to the Taylor family. Skinner and Eastwood's children were not interested in running the paper mill and also sold out to the Taylors. The Taylor family ran the paper mill for several years in conjunction with their two other paper mills and their large brickworks in the valley. Early this century, the valley mills were acquired by the Taylor's son-in-law, Robert Davies who was also involved in several large industries, including a brewery, elsewhere in Toronto. The paper mill at Todmorden became uneconomic in the face of the changes in papermaking technology that occurred around the turn of the century and was eventually closed and converted to provide stabling for the brickyard's large cart horses. Eventually it became the home of Whitewood's Riding Stables.

A brick road was constructed through the site when it became a stables to connect them to the brickyards and the houses in the valley were rented to brickyard employees. During World War II an internment camp for enemy aliens was constructed between the brickyards and the village site. I remember being told by a long-time resident of East York that these were very low-risk prisoners, mostly merchant seamen caught in Commonwealth ports when war was declared. The internees worked in the brickyards and, according to this same person, often socialized with their guards and residents of the community after work in the bar at the Todmorden Hotel at the top of Pottery Road hill. The camp burned shortly after the end of the war.

The construction of the Don Valley Parkway changed the terrain of the site enormously. The brick road's connection to the brickyard was cut, the mill-races were filled in, the course of portions of the Don River was changed and a hill of fill was dumped over much of the site of the internment camp. By the time True began promoting the site as the future home of the Borough's museum, the four remaining buildings were in very poor condition. The site was still unserviced by either sewers or other water service and providing these services proved to be among the project's greatest expenses—prompting some rather unpleasant questioning about what sort of luxuries were being installed down there. I remember seeing, in the Todmorden collection, a photocopy of one political cartoon from an unknown newspaper, which portrayed True acting sophisticated and artsy, talking in French to the project architect about whether they should really let the ordinary public use what the drawing described as the "Taj-mah-John." I wouldn't be in the least surprised if True put it into the collection personally, laughing along with it as she did so.

This cartoon captured more, however, than the debate over the cost of sewers for Todmorden in its portrayal of True as someone who felt more sophisticated than those around her. Her attitude towards others—and towards East York—was often ambivalent. She was widely admired and respected for her friendly manner with all of her constituents. Peter Worthington said of her that "she never thought she was better than anyone else, never sought privileges ..."[2] Yet she also could be irritable and extremely impatient with those she felt were plodding or mediocre; especially her colleagues on Council. Her habit of sighing loudly when impatient or exasperated was felt by some to express virtual contempt—even disdain.

Many of the attributes that she valued and praised about East

Todmorden Mills was East York's Centennial project and True's pride and joy. She is shown here with Peter Stokes, the project's restoration architect in 1966. *Photo by Ilse Mansfield, courtesy the Todmorden Mills Heritage Museum and Arts Centre*

York also irritated her. She praised its small town sense of community and "liked its good manners, its modesty, its smallness...but disliked its dullness...its lack of ambition and almost smug self-satisfaction."[3] Just as she had argued while on school board that all the students should be challenged to excell, that there was no such thing as good enough, she felt it part of her role as Mayor to challenge and provide intellectual stimulation for the people of East York in an effort to elevate its cultural and intellectual life. Her many admirers respected this as another example of her high standards, but as the cartoon illustrates, others were insulted.

True's campaign for Todmorden took several years of lobbying and negotiation before any work could begin. Doris Tucker remembered the course of True's efforts well.

> True Davidson was a woman of ideas, some great, some not so great. She was constantly challenging those around her. I can recall when...she decided that we should be starting to make plans for celebrating the centennial year. Most of us were so caught up in the day to day tasks we hadn't given any thought to centennial year. True, however, was determined that East York should have a head start on the other municipalities in Metropolitan Toronto, so as early as 1964 she called a number of citizens and staff together to formulate plans....About 1965 or 1966 the various governments announced that they would be prepared to make grants to municipalities for suitable centennial projects. As soon as this information was received True was busy seeking ideas for possible projects. You may recall that after Hurricane Hazel the Don Valley was proclaimed a flood plain area and buildings located there could longer be occupied as residences....the Metropolitan Toronto and Area Conservation Authority was established, and considerable work was done...[to prevent a similar disaster in future]. On the Authority's property, and situated in East York off Pottery Road were two old houses and an old brewery, along with the former paper mill. All in a terrible state of disrepair....True thought this would be an ideal spot for a historic site, so she started to promote the idea of making this a centennial project. At first she had great difficulty persuading anyone that this was a feasible idea. But never one to give up she talked about it wherever she could and eventually some of the [provincial] officials became interested. When she found she had an ally there she went to work on the Council. You know, in those days few people were interested in preserving old buildings. Eventually, her persistence won out. ...Council agreed...and once the grants were approved and Metro Toronto and the Authority had agreed to a 99 year lease, we were on our way.[4]

Willis Blair said that True's "main claim to fame was her sense of history. She was involved in saving Old City Hall and, of course, Todmorden Mills. We were 4-3 votes on a lot of that [the Todmorden project] but I guess we were one of the few genuinely Centennial projects and we're proud of it now." Charlotte Maher remembered fondly how proud True was of "her" museum. "She thought she was Todmorden Mills," and recalled when later "she found the railroad station somewhere and thought it was great." In a speech she gave to the Kiwanis, True expressed some of this pride, "Our Centennial project won province-wide, nay Dominion-wide, acclaim for its conservation of our natural environment along with our historic past."[5] She was always full of plans for the project and wasn't discouraged that funds had proved inadequate to permit the restoration of the paper mill. She was confident that "the frills can come later as we interest the public in the project."[6]

She wanted the museum to teach the history of the Don Valley from prehistoric times to the present. The brewery was intended to become a club room and information centre, to be used by the Don Valley Art Club and to display a collection of paintings of disappearing Toronto scenes. This building was later used for the museum's general exhibits, offices and archives. When the paper mill was renovated several years later, the Don Valley Art Club moved their clubhouse into a portion of it. True's dream of a theatre at the mills was fulfilled shortly before her death when the East Side Players Theatre moved into the two-storey portion of the renovated paper mill.

Peter Stokes was hired as restoration architect and Mrs. Nell Donaldson as the furnishings expert for the 1967 project which saw the two houses restored and furnished with an excellent collection of 19th century artifacts. The Don Train Station from Queen and River Streets was moved to the site later to save it from demolition.

True intended the site to be more than just a museum. She hoped to re-establish the trillium banks destroyed by the construction of the Don Valley Parkway and persuaded the East York Horticultural Society to plant and care for authentic old-fashioned gardens. The Iris Society installed a special planting of Canadian iris, which she felt would make "this project a real attraction even if we go no further."

Fantasy Farm expressed interest in operating a period restaurant in the old paper mill and True was sure that it would "be a financial success almost from the beginning." She hoped that, if the paper mill were ready in 1967, to persuade the Toronto Workshop Productions to establish their theatre there. Doris Tucker remembered True as a very strong supporter of the Toronto Workshop

Productions and thought she may even have helped to get it started. "When they had a play on, they'd call her and go there supporting them. She was always supporting the Arts."

Even though many of her schemes for the complex, including the period restaurant, came to naught because of the lack of adequate funds, True never stopped supporting Todmorden. Appointed Honorary Curator, she spent many weekends on site showing people around. She solicited artifacts from throughout the Borough and from descendents of the original families. She gave generously from her own possessions and bought several items that were needed to complete the period rooms after the government money ran out. She was always ready to take part in the site's special events, especially its Simcoe Day re-enactments. One memorable year, the newspapers reported that the "ghost of John Simcoe was late and True Davidson was annoyed."

> The ghost of John Graves Simcoe materialized in East York yesterday—but not until borough mayor True Davidson muttered, "Where the hell is he?"
>
> It was all part of East York's Simcoe Day at Todmorden Mills...and Miss Davidson, clad in a long green gown portrayed "The Spirit of the Don" to invoke the ghost of Simcoe, first lieutenant-governor of Upper Canada.
>
> "Listen for the fife and drum for when you hear it then he will come," she intoned. But the ghost was late and the mayor was annoyed.
>
> Finally, Simcoe did arrive—portrayed by Major Michael Stevenson, second-in-command of the Queen's York Rangers—but only a drumbeat heralded his late arrival....The families of the Todmorden community, dressed in period costumes, greeted "Governor and Mrs. Simcoe" and children.
>
> ...Governor Simcoe commented on the "shocking" condition of the Don River, nothing that his family once rowed six miles upriver to visit friends.
>
> "In those days it was crystal-clear water. I bought 300 acres of land and ordered that it not be spoiled but all that is changed," the governor's ghost lamented.
>
> The vice-regal party then enjoyed some home-made bread which The Spirit of the Don said she baked herself.[7]

A very windblown True in her Centennial costume with The Hon. Judy
LaMarsh, at the official opening of the Todmorden Mills Museum, 1967.
Courtesy the Todmorden Mills Heritage Museum and Arts Centre

The next year she played it safer, simply reviewing the Queen's
York Rangers' historical re-enactment guard wearing her pink silk
Centennial costume.

This wasn't the only time True blurted out her frustration
about delays during programmes at Todmorden. Before the site
opened, she had contacted many descendents of the Terry family
and invited them to participate. Mary Barnstaple remembered
that "my mother, father and several aunts and uncles were invited
to the official opening ceremony, at which "Governor Simcoe"
and a military band were supposed to participate. True, getting
very impatient, and forgetting her microphone was turned on, said
"Where the hell's the band?" which of course was broadcast all
over the valley."[8]

I well remember her plan to create an honour grove of trees
around Todmorden. She persuaded twenty-five groups and individuals to purchase the trees in honour of the Borough's "leading
citizens" but the Parks Department planted them around the
grounds instead of together because the soil where she had wanted
them placed was too full of rubble to permit them to grow. As

Curator-Manager of the site, I was charged with organizing the dedication ceremonies for the trees as part of the museum's official opening for the season. Not coming from a liturgical background but having read about the Rogation Service I asked the local minister to use it as the basis for his part in the service. The day dawned, cold and windy. The site's volunteer staff and I shivered as the skirts of our long "period dresses" blew wildly. True arrived and nearly left immediately when she discovered that the trees weren't planted in a grove, but was eventually persuaded to stay. The Opening Day parade, led by the Legion colour guard, marched down the hill, followed by a group of very young girl baton-twirlers, shivering in their extremely short skirts. Both groups were startled periodically by siren blasts from the fire truck that the Fire Department had agreed to send—if it could be at the back of the parade so it could leave instantly if it got a call! The Chair-

The Hon. Judy LaMarsh represented the Federal Government at the opening ceremonies. *Courtesy the Todmorden Mills Heritage Museum and Arts Centre*

man of the Museum Board spoke, True spoke, the baton-twirlers gave a demonstration then fled to the warmth of their parents' cars. The rest of us hugged our shawls around us and walked down to the parking lot where the largest clump of trees stood for the dedication service. It began to rain, and what a rain! Not a gentle spring shower—it poured and the wind drove it at us almost horizontally. My skirt and petticoats soaked through in minutes and clung soddenly to my legs as I heard the minister began the first Rogation prayer—a plea for rain! True stood throughout the ceremony, 73 years old, straight as the trees we were dedicating, sheltered by only a thin plastic rain coat and an umbrella which she could scarcely control.

Admirable as her continued support for the site was, I remember several members of the museum's Board of Management telling me in my early years at the site, shortly after True resigned as Mayor, that it could have a negative aspect as well. I was told on many occasions that my requests for repairs and additional staff "didn't stand a chance because the aldermen she used to make feel small knew that she loved the site and that they could hurt her by denying it." I never witnessed any direct corroboration of this revengeful act although my requests were routinely denied on the basis of insufficient funds. However, this was common in East York. The Borough's resources were small and appeals from municipal staff for additional budgets were seldom successful if there was any chance that it might increase taxes.

True actively campaigned against the proposed demolition of Old City Hall for the Eaton Centre. Her 1965 Christmas card exhorted its recipients on the subject.

> But our small friendly neighbourhood,
> In a great city complex caught,
> Cannot serenely stand aside
> Where there are battles to be fought.
>
> It matters greatly what is done
> With the old, mighty City Hall;
> the lands around the civic square
> Are surely vital to us all.
>
> ....
>
> If wealth demand the city hall,
> Wealth must have it. That is all
> The politicians dare to say.
>
> ....
>
> For if a man can pay
> Enough, there's nothing he cannot snatch away.
>
> ....

Are we the playthings of the men of power?
Or, in a splendid continuity,
Is there a challenge, a charge for you and me?
Perhaps this is the hour
Of destiny,
What kind of city shall our city be?[9]

True always believed that a city was made more by the activities of its citizens than by its bricks and mortar. She took great pride in the Borough's libraries, its winning high school football team "The Goliaths," its honour roll of Ontario Scholars, and "the talented young people who performed at the Sunday afternoon Musicales." She praised the work of the East Side Players, the Don Valley Art Club and "Mrs. MacDonald's theatre group at the Collegiate."[10] She told the Association of Mayors and Reeves that "I don't see why we can't have adequate cultural centres—libraries, art galleries, concert-halls, scattered across the province within reach of everyone. I'd like us to be able to travel enough to become truly bilingual and study enough history to be as proud of our French heritage as of our British, and interested in every other ethnic stock as well."[11] In an article written for *The East York News*, True admitted to wondering "why the council favoured building an open-air artificial ice rink, at a cost of $400,000, to be in service perhaps three months of the year but is so cautious about spending a few thousand for culture....Most of us don't do much skating in adult life, but things of the mind are a joy for ever."[12] Charlotte Maher recalled how "she liked paintings and she did a lot for the Foundation and the Symphony. East York wouldn't be East York if it wasn't for True. None of those, I believe, would have been flourishing. She didn't do them all but she certainly supported them."

Alan Redway remembered how difficult it was to say "No" to True when she wanted something to happen. Shortly after the amalgamation of East York and Leaside, she decided that the new municipality needed a new chain of office for the Mayor and began to approach all the service clubs in the community to contribute towards its purchase. Alan Redway was the President of the Leaside Lions Club at the time and remembered her phoning one day with this request. He declined, saying that the club really didn't have enough money to help out. "But True was never one to take no for an answer and she kept calling and pushing and eventually we found the money somehow."[13]

In order to enhance life in the Borough, True founded, and served as the first director, of the East York Foundation. The Foundation was established to serve as a non-governmental guardian of many of the Borough's treasures and as a fund-raising agency providing for cultural and recreational enrichment in fields which could not be covered by community taxation. She wrote of her efforts to raise money for the Centre for the Arts at Todmorden that "the Foundation will get the money somehow...and in years to come people may be prouder of...these things that have been done by voluntary effort than of the things which have involved large public expenditure."[14] Among True's greatest contributions to East York was her ability to inspire and attract intelligent and dedicated people to serve on the Borough's various Boards and Committees. Indeed some would say that this was one of her greatest strengths, since she was usually too busy, too involved in other, newer projects, and temperamentally unsuited to provide day-to-day supervision of any project for long.

Over the years, the East York Foundation has achieved many of True's dreams for the Borough, raising the funds for arts and cultural activities that, increasingly, have been unavailable from government sources. By providing a means of channelling bequests and other donations from individuals back into the community, the Foundation successfully raised much of the money needed to renovate the paper mill at Todmorden into an art gallery and community theatre; collected a sizeable collection of art by local artists including several works by members of the Group of Seven; provided funds to restore and exhibit some of the Borough's greatest treasures; and continue to provide financial assistance to publishers producing books about the community; as well as supporting numerous other community projects.

True was always available to speak to any group about the projects and issues that interested her and Doris Tucker remembered how people would call the next day and say "Oh, True Davidson made a wonderful speech the other night. Do you suppose I could get a copy? So I'd say, "We'll see what we can do. Was she looking at her notes? "Oh no, she was just talking off the cuff." And I'd say, "Well you'll have to get her cuff then." But sometimes she'd come and dictate it again. She'd remember what she'd said and

Muriel [Tozer] would type it up again ready for publication."

In 1967, True attended a conference, the Centennial Study and Trustee Programme on Metro Problems, which influenced her greatly. She reported hearing Beland Honderich say that "A city should be built to give its inhabitants security and happiness, " and that another speaker argued that for "over a million of more years [humans] learned to live in a more or less natural environment...living in family or tribal groups. ...His life in cities has lasted only a few thousand years and...he

True at microphone on the Todmorden Museum site. *Courtesy the Todmorden Mills Heritage Museum and Arts Centre*

has never been able to make a satisfactory adjustment to it" and "that there was need for much more research on the biology of Metropolitan areas." The same speaker quoted the United Nations code of human rights which declares that "Every man is entitled to be assured of a life whose level ensures health and well-being for himself and his family."[15] Other speakers dealt with the more traditional views of public health, but True was fascinated by this "Healthy City" concept. She reported telling a member of the American delegation who remarked that "Man is the most adaptable creature in the world and can adapt to all these problems of city life if he approaches them properly," "in my usual ferocious way" that "in the old days people used to be imprisoned in cages where they could neither stand upright nor lie down at night and managed to subsist for years, but that I did not consider this was really living." The conference reinforced her previously somewhat vague belief that "Cities can be beautiful and exciting, or they can be drab and soulless. They can be places in which [man] will find himself or places in which he will destroy himself. If they are to be good places to live—places of health and well-being—they require the co-operation of all." She broke this co-operation down into three categories: Physical co-operation—sharing the road, being considerate of the property of others, etc.; Intellectual co-operation—electing good representatives, studying issues and expressing informed opinions, thinking about the larger issues, teaching children discipline by personal example; and Moral co-operation—taking an interest in the community "for it is by serving others that we make ourselves happy and at the same time build a community." 16

True maintained her involvement with the University Women's Club, organizing among other programmes, their Twelfth Night celebrations. Emily Smith remembered that "she had us doing plays from the originals. The trouble is that it needed somebody like True to maintain that kind of thing."

These were the years of her greatest influence outside of the Borough. Joyce Crook, a life-long East York resident, remembered meeting True in Eaton's Annex "just after the time of the introduction of the new maple leaf flag. She had written to Premier Davis urging him to create a flag for Ontario by using our Red Ensign. This flag, she pointed out, was first introduced by Sir John A. MacDonald and represented with distinction our Canadian Forces in both World Wars. She was very proud of the fact that the Premier did accept her idea, making a few minor changes, but using the basic design for our Ontario flag."17 She had become accustomed to telling Premiers what to do. Clara Thomas remembered hearing John Robarts (then York's Chancellor) say "in his famous growl, "True used to come in through a secret door at Queen's Park and give me good advice."18

With her steadier income as Mayor, True bought herself a new house on Woodmount Avenue. This house still stands, unmarked and privately owned. Warren Gerard described it as a "comfortable home...On the wall is a brooding A.Y. Jackson forest and lake landscape and over the fireplace is a large dated oil of the Toronto landscape as seen from the Islands. The chairs are comfortable. Along one wall are built-in bookshelves and on one shelf is a magnificent Italian china piece of St. George slaying the dragon. It would have cost $500, but True got a bargain at Eaton's because a few of the dragon's teeth were chipped. In the adjoining room, the dining room, is the grandfather clock with the Westminster chimes that strike every 15 minutes. It is a comfortable home and True is at ease."[19] Gerard saw it at its best.

Jack Christie remembered it as always cluttered. "There were piles of papers everywhere." Her nephew, Michael, remembered that True entertained a lot as part of her position as Mayor, having frequent dinner parties and even more frequent tea parties. "She must have owned 100 dishes and they all just got left on the counter and her cleaning woman would come in on Monday and face this mountain of dishes as her first task." Emily Smith remembered it as being absolutely full of books and newspapers and other things associated with her career and said that True was never a good housekeeper. Charlotte Maher knew True in her final years and her memories of the house were even worse. "The place smelled and there were cockroaches and so much stuff." True just didn't have time or interest for what she described as "the sheer minimum of meal-getting, bed-making, laundry, etc., that permit[s] me to live."[20]

These years also brought her the joy of reunion with her nephews. She helped expedite their decision to come to Canada from South Africa in 1969, after thoroughly warning them of the difficulties they might encounter in settling here and finding work.[21] Charlotte Maher remembered that "she liked them both and I think she liked the idea of having nephews here but I don't think she was warm and giving to them. Everything was on an intellectual level." True's nephew David, remembered that she didn't really seem to warm up to him until just before her death. It is likely that she found suddenly having close family members living nearby again required considerable emotional adjustment.

True had grown up to be almost unnaturally close to her parents and sister. But they had all died years ago. She had cared and provided for the parents and suffered deeply when they died. Since then she had become accustomed to maintaining an emotional detachment from people, to being able to push them away when they started to get too close. She had successfully guarded her private life, her resentments and her self-doubt. Family, especially family who were now helping to look after her, had the potential of finding their way inside that guard and she wasn't sure she wanted to lose that detachment. Her nephews persisted—perhaps a Davidson trait—and, with time, she softened and became very fond of them and their children.

True served as President of the Association of Mayors and Reeves of Ontario in 1969—a year she described as "a busy one, but interesting and challenging"—filled with a multitude of reports to study, representations to make and numerous regional meetings. She warned the members that the municipalities of Ontario were at a crossroads where their powers were threatened by a province that was seeking to take back powers they had acquired over time. "For a century after the Baldwin Act of 1849, the responsibilities of municipalities slowly increased, as did the powers to enable them to meet these responsibilities. In the last two decades the trend has been reversed. There has been a gradual erosion of our powers and a weakening of our status. If this is not arrested, the end of the century may well find Ontario criss-crossed by networks of administrative districts operating directly under various department of the Provincial Government. These districts would be dominated by civil servants, with local elected people...serving mainly for the collection and distribution of taxes in accordance with their demands."[22] It is interesting to consider what she might have to say, if she were still around, about the present re-alignment of powers, responsibilities and funding arrangements that is being imposed by the present provincial government.

True reported to the membership of the Association that she had attended "39 committee meetings, 3 executive meetings, 9 meetings with the Prime Minister of Ontario and members of his Cabinet, 4 meetings with Special Committees of the Legislature and 2 with the executive of the C.F.M.M., where I represent this body. That makes 57 several engagements."

Having completed the list of activities for the year, she took advantage of what she called "the privilege of persons dying or retiring from office to give good advice to their successors." This "privilege" was one that she exercised more and more frequently during her final years in office as she tried to assess the value of her life and career by defining her beliefs and philosophies.

She told them that municipal leaders had to realize that Canada had changed from a pioneering country to a highly organized, industrialized society, with one of the highest standards of living in the world. "The pioneer virtues of hard work, courage, thrift, and mutual loyalty no longer seem relevant...We value things more than people.... We're on the skids. But we don't need to stay on them. All we need is to know what kind of world we want and to make up our minds we're going to have it." She then told them what she wanted.

"I want a world in which there are clean air, pure water, good food at reasonable prices and widely varied forms of modest shelter. I want a world that's healthy mentally and morally—not plagued by lust, violence, and all sorts of sickening perversions and addictions.

She said "it has long been my conviction that the average level of common sense and public spirit among municipal elected people is higher than on any other level of government, because the people know for whom they are voting and what they expect us to do." She then listed what she believed people wanted.

They want security. They want the protection of the police. But they do not want a police state. Civilian control of the police...is a matter of constant communication and mutual respect. We should continue to insist on this until we get it. Similarly, the people want Fire protection, but they don't want a multiplicity of expensive building regulations putting in fire doors which are always kept open...They want houses to be built to reasonable standards but not building codes which make it impossible to build homes for low income families.

She concluded her report with a call to "stop the erosion of municipal powers, because these are the people's powers, and because only at the municipal level can they see how the cost of meeting their demands increases their taxes....As long as we maintain conditions of public health, sanitation and public safety so as not to threaten our neighbours, we should be able to do so by whatever methods our communities prefer....With...municipal powers should come the establishment of proper tax bases...No proper planning and development are possible in our present state of financial insecurity. We are subject to a series of whimsical regulations which are changed without notice, often completely upsetting our budgets after our tax rate is set. Responsibilities are imposed or removed without prior consultation or even sometimes rational explanation. ...It must end."

11

THE GRANDMOTHER

OF EAST YORK

1969–1972

*T*rue's final term on Council began badly. She had considered not running again after the 1966 campaign because she had been in poor health "and it was a very unpleasant election" but changed her mind saying "I feel better than I have in 10 years" and "everyone seems to want me to run. They say East York wouldn't be East York without me."

Her opponent was once again Roy Brigham. Willis Blair considered running but decided to wait for the 1972 campaign. Concern was expressed by a Leaside aldermanic candidate that some of his constituents had "lost interest since the merger" of Leaside and East York. True responded by saying that "Council has been more than fair" to Leaside—a statement scarcely designed to sooth still ruffled feelings in that area.[1]

Although True claimed that she was in "fighting-trim"[2] Willis Blair remembered that she had been so ill prior to the election that "there was a meeting among some of us to determine what would be the status if she died during the election. I was being urged to run but if I lost and True had then died in office, I wouldn't have been eligible to replace her."

The campaign ended with cries of foul play by both sides. True charged that "a particularly vicious campaign" had been waged against her. "They would make everyone think I'm a ferocious tiger ready to devour everyone. It was a personal and sometimes whispering attack that was almost impossible for me to reply to in public." Her opponent, Royden Brigham, claimed that there were a "great deal of irregularities." His election agent, Joseph Bond, said that picture posters of Mayor Davidson were displayed in some polling sub-divisions and that he and his colleagues had been refused their rights as agents to look over the voting list at some polls. "I couldn't believe it but it was so," Bond was quoted as saying. "I've been in Montreal elections and thought they were bad, but I've never seen anything like that there."[3]

True won the election, but started to find parts of the job boring. Warren Gerard described her at a mid-term Council meeting.

She sat dolefully in the black leather chair at the centre of the horse-shoe table under the colored photograph of the Queen. They had said the Lord's Prayer. They had adopted the minutes of the last meeting and they were accepting nuggets of banality under the agenda heading of Communications: "From the Works Commissioner, submitting the Annual Report of the Senior Inspector under the Trench Excavators' Protection Act as required under Section 6a of such Act.

It is like this much of the time at East York council. Today its members are plodding from one dull, tedious item to the next, as if on a mission of gravity. Slowly, almost painfully, the tinkertoy housekeeping of Metro's smallest borough is being done. An audience of five watches.

And sitting in her black leather chair, wearing a big floppy black and white hat, sits the mayor and monarch of all East York: True Davidson. She looks every minute of 69. The eyes are closed (probably from boredom) while her court of eight male aldermen buzz around her like drones around a moody killer queen bee.

In fact, she looks more dead than alive. Her brown eyes are closed and the blue-black bags under them are sharply accented. Her angular, drawn face is deeply lined—a face that is beyond ugliness or beauty: it is a striking face....Now and then she twitches impatiently and somberly eyes her aldermen with restrained haughtiness and they race on in the word game.[4]

She had no more real competitors—everyone knew that this would be her last term as Mayor, even though she continued to threaten to run again. Gerard wrote that "True's colleagues and

Photographed during one of her many public functions. *Courtesy Jack Christie*

foes view her with bitterness and grudging admiration. She has never been defeated at the polls. And she hangs on....Her political foes compare her with John Diefenbaker, a man whom she greatly admires, and what East York needs now, they say, is a Dalton Camp."[5]

She still enjoyed the public role of being Mayor—of being "the grandmother of East York" and the newspapers still enjoyed reporting on her public functions. She was always good for a photograph or a quote. She wrote her name in the concrete of new apartment buildings, cut the ribbon at the opening of a branch of Centennial College in the Thorncliffe Plaza, and attended birthdays, wedding anniversaries and christenings.[6]

One of her efforts, an attempt to win the Red Cross Mayor's blood donor clinic trophy, made headlines and gave East Yorkers a vision of themselves that they liked. After a full day at work, True went to give blood at the clinic for East York. She lied about her age, but was rejected because of the heart medication she was taking. She went right back to the office and ordered a loudspeaker truck in which she was driven up and down the streets of the Borough, urging people to come out and donate. "For two hours, True Davidson pleaded to the citizens in the little homes and little shops and they locked their doors, got in their cars and came and gave. At 9:30...the Red Cross tabulated the results. The people of East York gave 359 pints of blood. Their quota was 200 pints. They scored a whopping 179 per cent."

She told another reporter that she delighted in attending high school commencements, and finding a job or a home for someone in a crisis. "There's not a day passes but you feel you've accomplished something. Maybe if I hadn't been here we wouldn't have the little parks, the playgrounds. There's nothing in the books to show what you've done because you don't make the motions. There's the long process of wearing down the opposition. But we've improved Pottery Road and we have an art gallery and even the little fountain in the hall (of the municipal office.) All over the place there are little somethings."[7]

Whether she always felt that these little victories were totally satisfactory is somewhat debatable. Her nephew, Michael, felt that True was ambivalent at times about her role as the mayor of Metropolitan Toronto's smallest municipality—that she sometimes felt that she had the ability to have played a more prominent role on the political stage than her "bit part" as Mayor of East York. He said he thought she sometimes looked at Chairman Gardiner and thought "why is *he* there and me here."[8] She was never satisfied with second-best, in others or herself, so it is likely that she did have times when felt dissatisfied with her accomplishments, but now even these—to which she had devoted herself to for more than 20 years—were about to end and she knew that she needed something else to replace it.

Her faith had never been easy or uncomplicated. Her nephew, Michael, described it as "tangled" but it had given her strength and emotional support at many times through her life. Now she found that even it was changing. She told an interviewer that "I had been dragging myself to church occasionally. My subscription was behind. It was very far behind. I was filled with a sense of shame to think that I had been stopping my support of the church because I wasn't getting any spiritual sustenance from it. To me the problem with the church today is that it has forgotten what it is supposed to be doing. It's supposed to be keeping the flame burning brightly in our hearts and it's not supposed to be changing the world. It's supposed to be changing us. Then we can go out and change the world. You see."[9]

Her nephew, Michael Cobden, remembers that she frequently came home from church in a state of exasperation, criticizing the sermon as mentally unchallenging and frustrated by its lack of the intellectual clarity that her father had taught her to expect.[10] Nina

Roberts remembered that around this time True had wanted to go and see the minister who had been at Woodbine Church but who had gone to another church well up north of the city and so she asked Nina's husband, Bill, to drive her. "Anyway. True wanted to talk to this minister. He was one of the old type of minister...the new one wasn't quite what she was used to. Shortly after we got up there it became obvious that she wanted to talk to him by herself so we went off and chatted with his wife awhile, you know, and after a bit she came out and we all talked for awhile. When we were getting ready to go, he said quietly to me, "She's one of the loneliest people I know." She was too. There were so few she could trust...and even them she seemed to share only little bits with."

Perhaps he helped. Certainly she began to express her faith more openly, perhaps hoping that in convincing others, she could retain it for herself. "It's been said that Christianity has been tried, and failed, and then somebody said : "Well, that's not true. It's just been found difficult and not tried." So I believe this now. I'm far from saying that I'm capable of living up to my Christian duty, but I certainly feel that I can try in a more public way."[11] Nina remembered that their church, Woodbine United, was one of the few places where True felt completely accepted for herself and not for her position. "She had been in the church so long. So no one thought when she came in "Oh, there's the Mayor," it was just "Oh, there's True." It was a real personal thing and that's nice."

True wrote about her feelings for this church in one of her newspaper columns.

> If I could give just one gift to the children of the world, I would give them God. God for the moment of anguish. God for the dullness of everyday. Last Sunday I was tired and sick but I wanted to go to church because my parents had given me a habit, a feeling that Sunday services are part of life. My church is small and plain. Our minister is not a great orator. Our music is often flawed, and when we introduce something special there are usually little unforeseen problems. But that church is full of love. It brims with it. It spills over.[12]

Despite all of her beliefs in the need for people to work together and to behave well to each other, True was always a difficult employer. In many ways, she duplicated the worst characteristics of the employers for whom she had worked for during her years in

business. She was de-
manding, critical and
could be extremely cut-
ting. I well remember the
whisper and scurry that
would occur in the office,
even after she retired,
when someone said,
"True is in the building."
Doris Tucker remembered
that, "Lots of times I had
little arguments with her
in the office there and I
really had to stand my
ground. But I always
made sure before I went
up there that I had all the
points set out clearly and
then I could stick to my
ground. I don't think she
ever said she was sorry."
She felt that True was unreasonable in her de-

Celebrating Canada's Centennial year "East York" style. *Courtesy Todmorden Mills Heritage Museum and Arts Centre*

mands of her secretary, Muriel Tozer,[13] "in a lot of ways." She was
infamous for waiting all day then "True would be going out that
night to speak and, at 4:00 in the afternoon, just when you'd be
thinking of going home, she'd be ready to dictate and she'd stand
over Muriel and dictate and Muriel would have to stay there and
type it up for her and I guess there were lots of changes and then
True would go out and speak and the paper would be in front of
her but nine times out of ten she wouldn't use it."   Doris felt that
True tried to make up for being so demanding and difficult by taking "her [Muriel] out for dinner, down to the Sutton Place, or if
there was anything on special. But I guess a lot of times, she just
wanted the company. I went too a few times. In her own way she
did make up for the times she sort of abused you although I can't
honestly say that she ever abused me. Maybe I stood up to her
better. Muriel, she'd just internalize it."..."She had a sharp tongue
but I used to sit down and I'd say to myself, 'Now how are we
going to handle this.' I had to remember that she was the head of

the municipality. I knew very well that with a person with a positive attitude like hers, you can't have her cow you. You have to stand up to her. Be polite, but this was the attitude I took."

She was hard on her friends too. June Callwood wrote that "She and I liked one another, though she felt perfectly free to dump on me on at least one occasion," but noted that "I always felt a lift when I saw her because her spirit was so thrilling...I loved her spunk."[14] Charlotte Maher felt True just didn't realize how deeply she hurt people who admired her and regarded her as a friend when she dropped them but expressed similar admiration for True's spirit.

Another public photo opportunity as the Mayor presents an award to a member of the East York Goliaths football team. *Courtesy Emily Smith*

Jack Christie's memories of working with True on Council were very similar to those of Doris Tucker. "If we made a point in a debate she would accept it—but she would never give out that she had. If I knew I had to go up against True on some issue, I would spend hours reading all the material so I was completely aware of all sides of that issue, to convince myself that my point of view was correct before I would oppose her. I didn't stand a chance otherwise."

The people of East York enjoyed hearing about how she dealt

with staff who failed to give good service. On one occasion, the water heater at an Eastdale Avenue apartment failed, and the superintendent referred the complaints to East York Hydro, which provided the service. "A hydro employee explained that the heater is in a box and only one serviceman has a key to it. Because that serviceman couldn't be found at home, 'nothing can be done.' *The Star* phoned Miss Davidson who said it was 'unbelievable,' and within minutes she had arranged for a serviceman to break the lock to fix the heater."[15] Her nephew, Michael Cobden, remembered one Easter Sunday when "someone called and said that their garbage hadn't been picked up. True got on the phone and called the Works Commissioner and told him to leave his Sunday dinner and go and pick it up. And he did."

Whether they would have approved of some of the stories about her behaviour towards some of the Borough staff is more questionable. Jim Lister wrote about one of the times he was assigned to chauffeur her to an evening event.

I recall one trip I made with True to the Toronto Hunt Club, on Kingston Road, for her to represent East York at a special dinner for representatives of all the Metro municipalities and the Province of Ontario. I picked her up at her home…at the appointed time and she was very much on edge. She said she must arrive at a specific time and be picked-up again at a specific time. So there was no leeway for deviation…. When we arrived at the Club there was a Government limo parked at the front door. I pulled up behind it and assumed she would get out. She turned to me and said "I am not getting out HERE, pull up to the DOOR." I said, "I can't Mayor, there is a car parked there." She said, "Well tell the driver to MOVE IT. So I got out and asked the driver of the Premier's car to pull up a bit, so my Mayor could walk straight in the front door. Which I did, which he did, which she did. All this the while she was giving me instructions to pick her up later at this DOOR, when she comes out. She did not say OR ELSE, but I got the message.

When I picked her up about 9:30 PM she was a different person, quiet and mild and so relaxed. She apologized for her manner previous, but said those big shots tried to intimidate her, and this made her edgy, being the only woman there. She also said, "I won't take this from them as I mean to be heard and have my say, as I represent the people of East York" [which she emphasized] "by banging her fist on the dash board.[16]

Difficult as he found her, Lister had great respect for True and was very loyal towards her. In her own way, True could be equally loyal to "her" staff. Jim Lister recalled another occasion when he had to drive her and an official from the Highways Department to see some new lights on the Allen Expressway when he had trouble getting onto the Allen because he was in the wrong lane. "The man from the Highways Department started to berate me which mixed me up even more. But Mayor Davidson jumped right in and told him off and to leave the driver alone, that I was HER driver and only SHE had the right to tell me WHATS WHAT. He shut right up." [17]

True loved working with children at events such as this fire safety promotion. *Courtesy East York Fire Department*

He also remembered the time that "one of the female clerks in the Tax Department came to work in a nice pant suit. The Clerk sent her home to change. Sometime, soon after, True wore a similar suit in. No one else was ever sent home, that was the end of that. I kind of think that True did it purposely, making a statement."

In 1971, True astonished everyone by deciding to run for the Liberals in that year's provincial election. She announced her intention to seek the nomination in February claiming, once again, that "I was always forced into politics, and I think my

True and Willis Blair attending the funeral of an unidentified East York employee. Courtesy *East York Fire Department*

friends greased the skids for me on this one. But now I love the idea."[18] Her opponent for the nomination, Donald Anderson, was shocked, exclaiming, "I'm amazed. She would be another Dr. Morton Shulman—an embarrassment to her party. [She's] like a kid who collects box tops [and this is her last box top.] It's fantastic and so out of character. She's the expert at putting out local brush fires and patching potholes, but I can't see her as a backbencher making two speeches a year."[19] True further shocked her constituents by claiming that she was "looking forward to holding the jobs of MPP and Mayor simultaneously."[20] She told Lewis Levendel from *The Toronto Star* that "physically, I am much younger than my years. Look at Churchill and Mackenzie King. Lots of statesmen were in their prime in their 70s." Asked how she would counter criticism about her suggestion that she would hold both jobs she replied, "My answer would be, 'Have I ever taken a job I did not do justice?' I have taken care of my health since I suffered a heart attack four years ago. I pace myself. I can work 15 hours a day but I don't let myself get excited." She went on to claim that "a spirit of adventure" had prompted her to seek the nomination. "It's like being ready to fall in love, like spring braking out inside you, feeling something new is going to happen."[21] Willis Blair remembered hearing that she hoped Trudeau would appoint her to the Senate if she ran a good race and lost, but "he never did."

Her declaration opened her up as a target for on the basis of her age, her East York parochialism and the suggestion that she would try and hold both jobs at once. She soon had to begin to step back from the idea of holding both jobs at the same time. "Oh, now, I didn't really insist that was going to stay on as mayor. After all, I haven't even been nominated provincially yet...and what would be the sense of definitely letting the younger men on council know I was stepping down? Why, they'd all be scrambling for the job and it would just create chaos."[22]

The newspapers continued to give her lots of ink, but the stories they selected increasingly reinforced one of these negatives about her. Thus, when they ran a story about her being given a senior citizen's card by the TTC at the Metro Council meeting, it reinforced the fact she was 70 year old, and when they told how "she owns a small car which she uses only occasionally. Normally she rides with the borough messenger on day-time business, a borough water meter reader at night—and has been known to hitch a ride on a works department truck if its going her way,"[23] she sounded small-town.

Then they reviewed her 70th birthday "bash" which they said was organized by "friends of Miss Davidson although one woman admitted that the York East Women's Liberal Association worked hard sending out 3,000 invitations and putting up posters publicizing the event."[24] Once again, this reinforced the knowledge of her age and made her seem manipulative—using the genuine good feeling of East Yorkers for political gain.

True was out of her depth in this new type of campaigning and wound up being accused by Metro Councillors of "electioneering" when she tried to introduce a motion in council criticizing Ontario's Conservative government.

She went for a fashion makeover with Stasia Evasuk, the *Star's* fashion writer, in tow. She wanted a new fashion image to go with her new political image, but instead reinforced people's perception of her age. I remember one of the museum volunteers laughing at the pictures of her after the makeover in a clipping we were filing, describing her her as looking like "mutton dressed as lamb."

Her campaign began well with suggestions that she was one of the Liberal's "election stars" and that she would doubtless get a cabinet seat once elected, but she was soundly beaten by the incumbent Conservative candidate, Arthur Meen. Charlotte Maher knew her at the time and remembered that "well-known and the incumbent" and said that "what did True in was that she wasn't one to do what she was told. They gave her this campaign manager, he was there all the time. They thought they had a real fish to fry there and he just struggled. She just would not do what he said. To a certain degree she was seeing it as just a little old East York Council campaign, but it was a pretty sophisticated campaign." This assessment is supported by True's campaign literature which stressed her local experiences and listed among her six primary goals, if elected, "Survival of an independent East York" and "Clean-up of the Don."[25]

After the election she claimed that she had known "back in March" that she wasn't going to win. "It went very much as I expected. I didn't think we had any chance of winning. I am too experienced a person not to know what we could do and could not do. I ran because I was so sick of what was going on at Queen's Park. There was too much money and too many other factors I don't want to go into...The Conservatives bought the people of Ontario with their own money."[26]

Disappointed in this opportunity, she had to begin to plan for her retirement. She flirted with the idea of running yet again for Mayor, saying "I would [give] my eye teeth to win just one term by acclamation. Just so I'd know there was once when everybody wanted me."[27] She had nearly equalled John Diefenbaker's record of election victories (10 in a row) and would have enjoyed matching him. But she had become eligible for a good pension and she was becoming more uncomfortable at Metro Council which she felt was becoming a rubber stamp for an increasingly centralized operation by the Metro Chairman's office. The Borough was changing from being "the most stable municipality in Metro, with very little turnover in its basically WASP, working-class population. [where] residents over 45 comprise[d] 38 per cent of the population...compared to just 19 per cent in...Scarborough."[28] Her eyeseight was deteriorating from cataracts and she had to start wearing glasses. Jack Christie said she knew "she was getting old and might be too old by the time she reached the end of the term. It was time for someone younger and she had been grooming Willis Blair for years." Willis was ready to run. He had backed off from running in 1969 when True declared her candidacy, but in 1972 he had declared his intention to run whatever she decided. He was quoted as saying, "But I would hate to run against True. She deserves to retire undefeated."[29] Willis told me that she decided against running when her long-time friend, Emily Smith, told her that "it was time to go and warned her that she wouldn't vote for her if she ran in 1972, she'd vote for Willis."

The decision was greeted with regret and almost a sense of relief by East Yorkers who, like Blair, wanted to see her leave with dignity. She resolved "not to become embroiled in any borough disputes until...[being] separated from my former job by at least two elections"[30] and set out to find a new inspiration to satisfy her during her final years.

12

AN ELDER OF THE TRIBE

1972–1978

*A*lthough not fated to enjoy her twenty years as an elder of the tribe, True wasted none of the time she was granted. She assured the Women's Canadian Club of Hamilton that she intended to enjoy life to its end. "I'm still drinking great gulps from the cup of life and I plan to keep doing so until I drain the last bitter-sweet dreg. But, many people leave not only the dregs, but some of the beverage, in their cup of life. Too many senior citizens stop living and organize to get more pension instead of more food for thought. Take life as it comes. Make the most of it. Fight against waste in life, as in other things. And when its over, be sure to drink up the sugar in the coffee cup."[1] On another occasion she wrote that "Old age, like youth, is a time of change, of innovation, of experimentation. That is why both periods can be painful and ecstatic. Youth is like the Dawn of Civilization; old age its Renaissance."[2]

She enjoyed the many testimonials and celebrations that surrounded her retirement, although she later criticized "farewell dinners [held] more for our own pleasure than for that of the dear departed."[3] The Borough named its new seniors residence, True Davidson Acres, after her. Its first administrator, Frank Russell, wrote to me of his experience with True around this time.

> I remember, with affection, how much she helped, in her own inimitable way, to get the Home's Volunteers recruited and organized late in 1972....A meeting was advertised in East York for an information session to introduce the Metro Homes in general and T.D.A.

in particular. Miss (as we knew her then) Davidson arranged for us
to meet at the old Municipal Offices and I did my "Rah! Rah!"
"what a noble enterprise" stuff to try to rally the troops. After some
minutes of this, Miss D. said something along the lines of "Young
man, this is all very interesting, but you should know that we East
Yorkers are doers not teachers. Tell these people, simply, what it is
you want, and if they like it, they'll do it!" Suitable chastened and
oriented to the East York way, I did just that and we had the start of
what turned out to be a dedicated group of Volunteers....I was
never sure just how much, if anything, it really meant to her to have
the Home named in her honour. I suspected that she had a sufficiently strong sense of who she was and the part she was playing in
the life of her Township that she felt no need for a monument.[4]

Immediately after her retirement, True began a new career as a
columnist and political commentator, writing occasional articles
for *The Toronto Star* and several local papers, providing occasional commentaries on CBC Radio and producing a twice-weekly
column for *The Toronto Sun*. A colleague of hers at the the *Sun*
wrote of her columns that she "crammed many ideas into each
piece, as thoughtful and restless intellectually in the Seventies as
she must have been as a girl."[5] Her nephew, David, remembered
how seriously she she took the responsibility for this column,
struggling to produce it regularly even after she entered hospital
for the last time. Although the topics for her columns covered a
wide gamut, their constant theme was the need for people to as-
sume personal responsibility for their own actions and to become
involved with the activities of government. In one month alone,
her topics ranged as widely as the issues surrounding child custody
cases, penal reform, unemployment insurance and the cause of
cutbacks in government funding. Writing of the problems of child
custody cases, she urged compulsory counselling before legal action was permitted and asserted that children were the responsibility of everyone in the community. "You see, a child really doesn't
belong to anyone. We all belong to the child."[6] Discussing how individual selfish actions, or even their carelessness and indifference
can harm others, she advocated that penal reform seek not to pun-
ish to encourage a desire to start afresh and that there was always
the possibility of atonement. "If the debt cannot be paid as in-
curred, it can be paid to another....We have all made mistakes that

have brought painful and costly consequences to ourselves and others. Nothing can change what the moving finger has already written, but it can write something better and brighter tomorrow. It is only if we continue to blot our copy, that the page should be torn out and thrown away."[7]

Writing about the problems with the unemployment insurance fund, she accepted some of the responsibility for the fact that because it had been used to fund social services as well as its stated purposes and thus couldn't establish accurate actuarial projections. "I was one of a delegation of mayors who besought the cabinet some years ago to extend the benefits, because the welfare burden was becoming intolerable, with free health care, free drugs, free dental care and other benefits constantly being added under pressure from the do-gooders, whom everybody seems afraid to question. We felt that unemployment insurance was more controllable. We didn't know what we were talking about. Or perhaps we did, and didn't care, so long as we could shelve some of our own burden."[8] She told her readers that because everyone wanted only the best without wondering how we could afford it, the political parties gave it to them without consideration of the economic consequences. "No matter how high the ideals of the individual candidate for election, the aim of the party is to get power and to keep it. It will bribe us with our own money in all sorts of indirect and perfectly legal ways....It will collect our money and redistribute it to us in ways which make economists and auditors shudder with horror....[then when cutbacks come] we squeal like stuck pigs. But we have been behaving like pigs....The only thing which can stop it is US!"[9]

Thus in the course of one month, she dealt with many of the issues we are struggling with now—more than twenty years later!

Peter Worthington remembered that he had been impressed by True:

When all (most) politicans were raving that Paul Rimstead running for Mayor in 1972 disrupted the democratic process [and] True was one of the few (along with David Crombie) who saw him as a genuine "protest" candidate who filled a need or gap that conventional policians didn't. I was editor of the fledgling *Sun* at the time & felt someone with her intellectual and moral courage, & her fearless defense and advocacy of her beliefs was the sort of columnist we needed in the *Sun*. I didn't care what her views were—just that they were truly held, well expressed, & even when she took an unexpected turn, they were valid & valuable.[10]

Worthington added that "I had great admiration (& affection) for True, but did not socialize with her & wasn't one of her cronies. I admired her independent spirit & felt she believed in all the tenets of justice, fair play, common sense, & she could look at things that affected her, politically & personally, with objectivity and dispassion."[11] Worthington's admiration and affection for True was shared by many prominent people, including many who did not often agree with her and even by many who suffered from her sharp criticism. I suspect that, like Worthington, they were personally big enough to recognize the honesty of her beliefs and to be able to consider them without threat to their own, equally honest, opinions.

True was one of the earliest advocate of environmentalism within the Toronto urban setting, claiming that "it appeared to me like the light before Paul on the road to Damascus that I should fight for the environment for the rest of my life. I was only 71 then."[12] She had always had a strong emotional attachment to the natural environment and was inspired by Charles Sauriol who had lived in the Don Valley and published his newsletter, *The Cardinal*, throughout her years on Council and who had worked with her on the Todmorden Mills project. True continued to serve on the Metropolitan Toronto and Region Conservation Authority after her retirement, and wrote and spoke on the subject seeking to "interest my fellow voters in the prudent ecological management which the wise and far-seeing tell us is absolutely necessary for the future of the race."[13] Helen Juhola, a prominent member of the Toronto Field Naturalists, remembered going to speak to True about one of her issues. Her previous impressions of True had been only that "she was a wierd woman who always wore a different hat" but she came away from the meeting with the realization that "she was one of the sharpest people she'd ever met. True heard us out, asked some very intelligent and relevant questions and eventually wrote an article in which she called us naive young things or words to that effect, but also wrote up the issue in a very supportive way. She didn't miss any of the important points."[14] True lived what she preached, taking home food scraps from luncheons to feed her cat, bringing her own bags when shopping, and recycling and composting so as to produce "only a handful of garbage each week."[15] These actions, so commonplace today, were then seen as extreme, almost the action of a crank, but True never hesitated to throw her reputation and her ability to get media coverage into the struggle for anything she believed to be worthwhile.

She continually urged her readers to live life to the full. Writing of Hugh MacLennan, she said that "the consciousness that life is good, that even a little of it is worth having and enjoying to the full runs through all of [his] work. We must take people as they are and life as it comes and death when we meet it. We can make all beautiful through courage and faith and tenderness. There is always a tomorrow for someone, a tomorrow which we can have helped to build."[16] She said that "age is a time of contemplation, a time to read and grow intellectually. If age doesn't bring wisdom, it means life has been pretty well wasted."[17]

Her book *The Golden Strings*, was published in 1973. Although many had wanted her to write an autobiography, she wrote instead of those who inspired her and especially of their activities near the end of their lives. Of herself, she wrote "I am growing old. I am half blind and no longer balance well...But my spirit—the essential me—is still as full of wonder and delight as that of a young girl. I do not want to become a placid observer on the banks of the stream. I want to stay in the current, thrill to the full pressure of life until death sweeps me over the falls. I do not want to cling abjectly to this bodily existence 'as though to breathe were life.' I am not afraid of what lies over the falls. But while I am still in the river of time I want to pull at least my own weight in the boat."[18] As always, her Christmas poem expressed her thoughts and concerns. Doris Tucker kept the following poem from one of True's last cards.

The old have much need to be patient;
The young have much need to be brave;
For the old have a wild world to manage
And the young have a sad world to save.

We can do it by working together
With love, understanding and trust;
These qualities chiefly are needed;
We can make them ours and we must.[19]

York University granted her an honorary doctorate in June 1978, presenting it to her in hospital. It read in part, "For two years, from 1975—1977, she honoured York University with her presence as a Ph.D. scholar in the Canadian literary field. Neither professors nor students will forget the challenge and the stimulation of her quick interest and her warm and witty presence. Now, York University wishes in its turn to honour True Davidson—a Great Lady, a Lifelong Scholar, a Canadian Patriot." She died three months later. *Courtesy Emily Smith*

In 1974, the Borough commissioned her to write a booklet about East York's history as part of its 50th anniversary celebrations. True, instead, set to work to produce a book and began missing deadlines as result. I remember hearing that many on Council were frustrated by what they regarded as her willful disregard of their instructions and that, eventually, they demanded that she surrender her draft text and notes. These, regrettably, were edited then into a small book, *The Golden Years of East York,* which is full of errors, both factual and typographical. True, understandably, refused to let them use her name as author but it is interesting to note that, in my copy, at least, her picture was glued opposite the title page, though there is no indication that she ever accepted authorship of the book.

True was full of plans for future books. She told one group that she planned to write one about the women in Canada's history. She contacted Garfield Evans who she had known in Streetsville many years before and who had since had a successful career as a Game Warden in Nipigon, to set up interviews for her with the local natives so she could write a book about them. "As a Game Warden, I knew all the old ones with stories to tell and I considered real friends. Arrangements were all set. She would stay with Iva and I in Nipigon & I would take her to the reserves to interview the people. Trust is a wonderful thing. I felt out some of the old characters and if she was a friends of mine, yes, they would talk to her." This project, like many, was not to be. As Mr. Evans wrote, "The next thing I know I get a phone call she is sick and the end wasn't too far away. So the world turns."[20]

The honours began to arrive. In 1971, Victoria College awarded her am honorary degree as a Doctor of Sacred Letters. In 1973 she received the Order of Canada, followed in 1977 by the Queen's Silver Jubilee Medal. Proud as she was of these honours, she was equally proud of being named "Citizen of the Year" by the East York Kiwanis. True also prized and carefully kept some of the letters she received around this time. Florence Deacon wrote to congratulate her on receiving the Order of Canada and told her that "it is a marvellous thing to see what can be done with a life; you have been an inspiration in so many ways to so many persons in the things you have done."[21] June Callwood wrote to tell her that she had put one of her columns on her wall "not so much because of the lucid writing and the intellectual perspective and the interesting reflections, but because it demonstrates something about grit and curiosity and responsibility and style that I admire in you...and want for myself. You are beloved to a great many people for a great many people. I just thought you should know that."[22] John Diefenbaker wrote to thank her for comments she made about him in her column adding "they are all the more important to me because of the fact that your contribution to public life throughout the years has been a distinguished and fruitful one."[23]

Her intellectual searching took many forms. She helped form the Sherlock Holmes Club, The Bootmakers. Their name is derived from a reference in *The Hound of the Baskervilles* to "Meyers, a bootmaker from Toronto." In 1975 she served as its president, who is always known as "Mr. Meyers." In the spirit of humorous study which characterizes The Bootmakers, she delivered a "learned article" full of mock scholarship and imaginery footnotes, "Seven Drops of Water, About Canada's Holmes," at one of their events which "proved" that Sherlock Holmes had been born at Fort Garry, Manitoba. She based her theory on the casual reference his biographer, Arthur Conan Doyle, makes to a marsh being so disturbed it looked as though a buffalo had wallowed there. "Now, I make the point that nobody born in England at that time would have said such a thing."[24] She drew press attention to the society during her years there, as to any other activity in which she became involved, being photographed wearing a deerstalker hat and in costume at a social outing of the club. This still thriving club honours True each each year by presenting the "True Davidson Memorial Award" for the best paper presented at a meeting of The Bootmakers.

She went back to university, seeking to get the PhD she had been unable to pursue 50 years before. She organized a special course of study in Canadian Literature and History where she "brooded over Quebec-English relations and, in her way, sought to reconcile the two solitudes."[25] Clara Thomas was one of her professors and remembered her as being "a great learner. She never stopped learning. She was fascinated by the perspectives of the young. I don't remember her ever criticizing any of them and yet there were things said that were quite alien to her time and thought, but she was learning all the time. New viewpoints were interesting to her." Clara considered writing a biography of True herself, but decided that she didn't know enough about her political career to do it justice. Instead she wrote a paper about her experiences with True at York which she generously gave me permission to use in this book.

One May day in 1974, Margaret Laurence and I went from our house to a Canada Day celebration in Hamilton. When I returned that evening, our son John, home from Queen's, handed me a sheaf of messages. "These are mostly from True Davidson," he said. "I don't know whether she wants to take your class or give it, but you'd better call her—right now." So I did and found that True was planning on registering for graduate work at York in the Fall, and planned to take my seminar on the Canadian novel, as well as Eli Mandel's on contemporary experiments in Canadian Literature. It was a memorable year! Probably the most memorable Grad course in all my years of teaching. I had about a dozen young Grad students from all over, Suan O'Heir, Associate Dean of Nursing at the U. of T., who had taken a leave of absence to do an M.A. in English, and

True. She had at that time had two cataract operations, and was always brought to the campus by her devoted friend and oft-time driver, Emily Smith. There was an initial session of polite distance on the part of the young students, but that was speedily dispelled, and soon they were treating her as a combination of favourite aunt and very special person, which she was.

True had a powerful personality, and a powerfully attractive presence, and we all reacted to it as in her past many a political committee-council-commission had reacted. She stunned us all by her working habits. The first topic she chose to give a seminar on was the Picaresque novel. She came, laden with books and references, and swept the table with her eyes: "Of course this all starts with the Spanish," she announced. "DON QUIXOTE you know. How many of you read Spanish?"

There were no responses. "Well," she announced, "It's quite simple. You just get a dictionary and translate." With which sweeping, and to them stunning, statement, she proceeded to translate various Spanish texts on the picaresque.[26]

Clara recalled that True was completely open to opinion and so did well in her literature classes but that problems developed in her history classes.

After my class and Eli's, which she also loved, she took several history classes. These didn't go as well as our English classes, I think because she did tend to sound off about her version of history—and of course she had lived through a gret deal of it. She also couldn't accept the way history is now taught, a very different technique from her days of schooling, when the assembling of data was the main thing, not the critical perspective that our historians cultivate. At any rate, her plans for a PhD finally crashed, and for a time, she told me, she was devastated.

Being True, however, she picked herself up, moved off the York campus where she had taken a bachelor apartment in the Atkinson Residence to be close to her work(when I saw it, the apartment was crowded with hats!) and made plans for travel to Australia and New Zealand.[27]

True was always unstoppable. John Downing remembered attending the United Nations "Habitat" Conference with her, "when True slipped and fell heavily amidst the Vancouver rush-hour traffic. She insisted that she could continue without going to hospital. But she couldn't walk. So I half-carried her up a long hill, along a street and up to two floors to a room where we had been told the Canadian delegation was meeting. The meeting had been moved to a downtown hotel. True insisted we had to go there. So I found a cab, loaded her, unloaded her at the hotel and carried her to the room. There were no chairs left as True swept imperiously in, no sign of pain on her face. But Hopalong [Michael] Cassidy, now Ontario's NDP leader, graciously gave True his. No sooner was she settled than she interrupted the speaker, Senator Ray Perrauld, with a criticism of the government position. She could have been a member of the counter culture movement, not a grandedame." Downing discovered the next day that she had fractured her pelvis. "I asked her how she was managing. I don't remember everyone she had pressed into service but it sounded as if the U.B.C. president was doing her shopping aided by the lieutenant-governor. She said she would still be off the next day for her first look at the Arctic Ocean. The wheelchair wouldn't be that much of a problem, she said."[28] Clara Thomas recalled this same courage. "The gallantry of it. Think of it. Going back to do a PhD after two cataract operations. Doing all that reading after two cataract operations."

True greatly enjoyed the opportunity to travel that retirement—and a pension—gave her. She visited Germany, where she saw the Oberammergau Passion Play and toured Yugoslavia including a visit to East York's twin city, Skopje. She had begun a tour of Australia and New Zealand when she fell and x-rays revealed a cancerous growth.

Determined at first not to let even this stop her she told Clara Thomas that "I think there must still be something for me to do, even at my age. There must be a reason, otherwise I wouldn't still be alive."[29] One of her obituaries noted "by God she was tough! She didn't go quietly, but kicking, protesting, planning for a future that wasn't to be."[30] Peter Worthington remembered that "even in hospital she was gutsy and humorous."[31] She knew that she was going to die. Willis Blair remembered that she asked him in July, two months before her death, to deliver her eulogy. She began to resign herself to the inevitable, quoting from Kipling, "He had been, as the Old Law recommends, 20 years a youth, 20 years a fighter…and 20 years head of a household. He had used his wealth and power for what he knew both to be worth; he had taken honour when it came his way; he had seen men and cities far and near, and men and cities had stood up and honoured him. Now he would let these things go, as a man drops the cloak he no longer needs."[32] She selected a prayer for her funeral, "God of strength, give me the fire to fight life's battle to the end...But God of mercy, give me steel to bear defeat if that is what you send."[33]

After her death, the True Davidson Collection of Canadian Literature at York University was established in her honour. The patrons of the collection included the Hon. Pauline McGibbon, then Lieutenant-Governor of Ontario, shown here at the official opening ceremony. *Courtesy Emily Smith*

She never stopped studying and thinking. Dalton Morrison remembered how "in hospital she turned her mind to the writings of Northrop Frye, often called Canada's greatest living scholar. One day I visited her True said, "Listen to this." She read a paragraph. "What does it mean?" "I don't know," I said. I waited for the blast. "Neither do I," she confided."[34] She remained as opinionated as ever. When Morrison was leaving her hospital room one day, True asked him to bring her a dictionary next time I came. "I said, 'I'll bring you a Webster,' and began my exit. 'You'll bring a what?' she challenged. 'I'll bring an Oxford,' I promised."[35] York University granted her an honorary doctorate in June 1978, presenting it to her in hospital. It read in part, "For two years, from 1975-1977, she honoured York University with her presence as a Ph.D. scholar in the Canadian literary field. Neither professors nor students will forget the challenge and the stimulation of her quick interest and her warm and witty presence. Now, York University wishes in its turn to honour True Davidson—a Great Lady, a Lifelong Scholar, a Canadian Patriot."[36]

But Charlotte Maher who stayed at the hospital with her nephew, Michael, until about 11:00 on the night True died felt that she eventually decided that it was time to give up. "I don't think I ever heard her say she regretted anything, but at the end she didn't want to be alive anymore so she was regretting being alive. She stopped eating and one of the nurses said that she shouldn't have died [when she did.] It wasn't cancer that killed her. If she couldn't do more interesting things in life she didn't want to continue."

True Davidson died on Monday, September 18, 1978. She was laid in state in the East York Council Chambers until her funeral. After cremation, her ashes were buried in the family plot at Union, near St. Thomas, Ontario, beside her parents and her sister. Willis Blair delivered the eulogy she had requested him to make to a church full of mourners—many of them weeping openly. Peter Worthington remembered "rushing to her funeral—I was a pallbearer— I was stopped on the Lakeshore for speeding—& when the cop learned why I was speeding, he gave me an escort to the Church. That indicates, I think, the sort of respect True generated."[37]

True's final poem revealed that she approached death with the same curiosity with which she faced life.

> I looked out of the great hospital windows
> With dying eyes
> And millions of stars spangled across the far
> And dark blue skies.
> They were not the reflections of the dazzling and dancing electric decorations—
> And I knew what lay between—
> The man-made murk of pollution and filth and waste and woefulness.
> They could not be seen.
> But I was dying and I saw them as they are there—
> They are there forever
> In the glory my childhood knew,
> The stars of love and hope and courage and beauty and honour.

And a not impossible You.
The eyes of the dying see what the living
Have no time to look at.
They see with something stronger and truer
Than temporal eyes.
Clear away the man-made miasma of dirty self-seeking
And see what God has written in the skies.[38]

A number of commemorative funds were started after her death, including a student scholarship in East York and the True Davidson Collection of Canadian Literature at York University which began with the books and papers she left to York University to be used to further Canadian Studies in English and in French. The patrons of the collection included the Lieutenant-Governor of Ontario, York University's President and its Chancellor, and many prominent politicians and scholars including Flora MacDonald, Doris Anderson, Beth Appledoorn, Isabel Bassett, Willis Blair, Pauline Jewett, William Kilbourn, Margaret Laurence, Mavor Moore and Edith Patterson Morrow. The co-ordinators were Clara Thomas and Edith Fowke. Margaret Laurence and Margaret Atwood helped to raise funds for the project by giving special readings at York. The fund raised more than $31,000 which was used to establish an important collection of books, manuscripts, journals and microfilm in the areas of literature and history at York.

As the days remaining for East York's existence as an independent municipality dwindled away in the face of the provincially-imposed amalgamation into the new Toronto "Megacity," Councillor Norm Crone approached Mayor Michael Prue to suggest that True Davidson be honoured at the final Council meeting.

Mayor Prue encouraged the idea and, at the October 7th Council meeting, Councillor Crone's original motion to name the Council Chambers in honour of True was passed unanimously.

On November 17, 1997 the East York Council Chamber was designated the True Davidson Council Chamber. Her formal portrait, painted by A. Good in 1971, was hung inside the chamber to remind all of her many contributions to East York.

The Mayor's chain of office presented to her by the service clubs of East York (the Lions, Kinsmen, Kiwanis and Rotary clubs) will remain in East York in the care of the East York Foundation, another of her creations.

Somehow I like to think that while True Davidson would mourn the loss of her beloved East York, she would be honoured by the recognition and pleased by the Council's decision to celebrate the municipality's history.

EPILOGUE

So now we return to the beginning. What can we "truly" say about True? She was so many different things to so many different people. No one knew the all of her—and even after two years of research I won't presume to suggest that I know her at all. The best I can do is to finish with the opinions of some of those who knew her.

Opponents characterized her sometimes as arrogant and selfish, but she devoted her whole life to her wide interests in history, civic affairs and conservation and to her constituents. She never had an unlisted telephone number.

The Globe and Mail, September 19, 1978

Flamboyant but never frivolous, cutting but never cruel, True Davidson enlivened municipal politics during her long tenure in office. She…bears emulating by any woman with political ambitions.

The Toronto Star, September 19, 1978

Decent, fearless, independent. True was a thorn in the flesh of the smooth men at Metro.

William Kilbourn, historian, author and
City of Toronto councillor

She was a very fine woman and even though she had a caustic tongue she was a friend of everyone. The people took to her because she was a champion of the people. Anytime people needed her, she was there.

William Roberts, Gledhill Avenue, East York

She had that mean streak, but the people loved her.

Unidentified mourner at True's funeral,
quoted by *The Toronto Star*

There was no quitter in her make-up and she fought like a banshee for whatever she believed in—which was people, truth, Canada. People either loved her or loathed her. None was indifferent. All her life True Davidson stood for human values. And traditions. Her courage and integrity knew no limit. She didn't make a cent from politics and scrimped and saved to make ends meet. She overflowed with opinions, ideas,even prejudices. She was a straight as they come.

The Toronto Sun, September 19, 1978

Those frilly hats camouflaged a clever, sometimes perverse, tongue and intellect. Her precise, biting words could rasp the veneer from an official at 10 paces, sneak through a loophole, and such the pomposity from a politician until he was reduced to a mewling baby. She was unique in a world where too many politicians have a cookie-cutter sameness. The Queen Bee surrounded by the drones. She was always true to herself—she was named well— never captive to party, colleague or lobby.

John Downing, *The Toronto Sun*

She was a fantastic woman. If we have brilliant people like that doing good things for us we're just going to be real lucky.

Emily Smith, her friend

There is no doubt about it, no one who was in East York then could say she wasn't fair or for the people whether it was the smallest detail or the biggest. If it was a problem with them it was a problem with her.

Nina Roberts, fellow member of Woodbine United Church

She was a wonderful woman, with a terrific presence and influence, and a role model many of us, including myself.

Professor Clara Thomas, York University

There are lots of stories about True, but I think she always cared for the little guy and I found her very fair to work for, though she did have her moments...I might add that East York being the so-called "smallest" municipality in Metro some thought they could take us for granted. NOT WITH TRUE DAVIDSON. She was a great representative for East York and got a great many things done.

                                        Jim Lister, retired East York employee

East York was her her pride. Everything that she did was for the betterment of East York. She was so proud of it. And I guess she had reason to be. The people sort of took her to heart and it was the only place she really felt at home.

                                Doris Tucker, Clerk (Ret.), Borough of East York

When I was 5 years old (1955) my Dad and I were driving to our home in East York. We stopped along another car at a traffic lite. I looked over the next car & said very loudly, "Look Daddy, a witch." The windows were down on both cars and Ms. Davidson & I were only inches apart. She smiled, waved and drove off. After my Dad had recovered from this embarrassing situation, he said "Remember how there were 2 witches in the Wizard of Oz? One good—one bad? Well, she may not be pretty but she's like the good witch in the movie, helping lots of people.
I never forgot his words and whenever I saw True Davidson, I remembered how much my Dad must have respected her—a woman ahead of her time.

                                                        Sandra Crowe

SOURCES

ARCHIVES

Metropolitan Toronto Reference Library, microfilm newspaper collection.
United Church of Canada/Victoria University Archives, Davidson and Pomeroy
    folders.
York University, Archives and Special Collections, True Davidson papers, 1978-004.

LETTERS TO THE AUTHOR

E-mail from Mary Barnstaple, December 27, 1996
June Callwood, September 24, 1997
Joyce Crook, December 2, 1996
Sandra Crowe, September 17, 1996
Tom Edwards, September 18, 1996
Garfield Evans, September 8, 1996
Gord Hazlett, November 27, 1996
Jim Lister, September 23, 1996
Joan I. Moore, September 16, 1996
Frank Russell, 1996
Peter Worthington, 1997

INTERVIEWS (Taped)

Willis Blair, 1997
David Cobden, 1996
Harry Evans, 1997
Charlotte Maher, 1997
Nina Roberts, 1996
Emily Smith, 1996
Clara Thomas, 1996
Doris Tucker, 1997
Reeta Wright, 1996

INTERVIEWS (By Telephone)

Jack Christie, 1996
Michael Cobden, 1996
Helen Juhola, 1997
Alan Redway, 1997

OTHER PRIMARY SOURCES

Newspaper clippings kept by Nina Roberts.
Website, http://www.net.gull-lake.sk.ca: 80/town/clubs/cgit/cgit.htm
Letter to Emily Smith from True Davidson, August 3, 1950
Christmas card sent to Doris Tucker by True Davidson, ca. 1977

SECONDARY SOURCES (Published)

The Canadian Encyclopedia, Second Edition, Hurtig Publishers: Edmonton, 1988
Crowley, Terry, *Agnes MacPhail and the Politics of Equality*, J. Lorimer: Toronto, 1990
Davidson, True, *The Golden Strings*, Griffin House: Toronto, 1973
Lipset, Seymour Martin, *Agrarian Socialism, The Cooperative Commonwealth Federation in Saskatchewan*, up-dated edition, Doubleday & Company, Inc.: New York, 1960.
Martyn, Lucy Booth, *Aristocratic Toronto: 19th Century Grandeur*, Gage Publishing: Toronto
McNaught, Kenneth, *A Prophet in Politics*, University of Toronto Press: Toronto, 1959
Pennington, Doris, *Agnes MacPhail: Reformer, Canada's First Female M.P.*, Simon & Pierre: Toronto, 1989
Torontoniensis, 1921
Young, Walter, *The Anatomy of a Party: the national CCF 1932-61*, University of Toronto Press: Toronto, 1969

SECONDARY SOURCES (Unpublished)

Morris, Dalton A., "Funeral Tribute for True Davidson," September 21, 1978
Thomas, Clara, "A Memoir of True"
Tucker, Doris, "Text for a talk given at Central Park Lodge," November 1990

NOTES

CHAPTER 1 A CHILD OF CANADA

1 Newspaper clipping, paper unidentified, February 14, 1968, headed 'Only Had Year to Live', So True Entered Politics, York University Archives, 1978–004/11B

2 Brian Swarbrick, 'Just Plain True' Davidson is Ready to Begin a Brand New Career at 70,'*The Toronto Star*, Saturday, March 13, 1971

3 Newspaper clipping, ca. 1928, "Its Literature Can Do Much to Benefit Canada," unidentified Barrie newspaper, Archives and Special Collections, York University, 1978–004/03

4 Brian Swarbrick, "'Just Plain True' Davidson Is Ready To Begin A Brand New Career at 70," *The Toronto Star*, March 13, 1971

5 Letters of reference 1922–1925, Archives and Special Collections, York University, 1978–004/11

6 *Torontoniensis*, 1921, Archives and Special Collections, York University, 1978–004/12

7 Letters from Office of the Recording Dean, Bryn Mayr College, Pennsylvania to Miss Davidson, April 14–30, 1925, Archives and Special Collections, York University, 1978–004/11

8 Taped interview with Charlotte Maher, 1997. Further references will not be footnoted unless the source is unidentified in text.

9 "Trinity of Interests Meet in Women's Canadian Club," newspaper clipping, unknown paper, date almost certainly April 15, 1931, Archives and Special Collections, York University, 1978–004/03

10 Draft for her column in the *Toronto Sun*, Archives and Special Collections, 1978–004/02B

11 "Tried and True", *The Toronto Sun*, September 19, 1978

12 Terry Crowley, *Agnes MacPhail and the Politics of Equality,* (J. Lorimer: Toronto), 1990, p. 9

13 United Church of Canada/Victoria University, "Record of Service", John Wilson Davidson and "Obituary," Hamilton Conference, Minutes 1941

14 Warren Gerard, "True Davidson, Monarch of all East York", *The Globe Magazine,*March 13, 1971

15 True Davidson, *The Golden Strings,* (Griffin House: Toronto), 1973.

16 Warren Gerard, "True Davidson, Monarch of All East York," *The Globe Magazine*, March 13, 1971

17 Column by True Davidson, *The Toronto Sun*, date unknown, from clippings kept by Nina Roberts

18 True Davidson, "The Philistine Years," *The New Outlook*, December 31, 1930, Archives and Special Collections, York University, 1978–004/03

19 Ibid

20 Warren Gerard, "True Davidson, Monarch of All East York," *The Globe Magazine*, March 13, 1971.

21 United Church of Canada/Victoria University, "Methodist Church (Canada) Obituary," Methodist Church Toronto Conference Minutes, 1920.

22 Telephone interview with Michael Cobden, 1996. Further references to this interview will not be footnoted unless the source is not acknowledged in the text.

23 Taped interview with Doris Tucker, 1997. Further references will not be footnoted unless the source is not acknowledged in the text.

24 Column by John Downing, *The Toronto Sun*, September 19, 1978

25 True Davidson, "The Philistine Years," *The New Outlook*, December 31, 1930, Archives and Special Collections, York University, 1978–004/03

26 Warren Gerard, "True Davidson, Monarch of all East York," *The Globe Magazine*, March 13, 1971.

27 Taped interview with Clara Thomas, 1996. Further references to this interview will not be footnoted unless the source is not acknowledged in the text.

28 Warren Gerard, "True Davidson, Monarch of all East York," *The Globe Magazine*, March 13, 1971.

29 Taped interview with David Cobden, 1996. Further references to this interview will not footnoted unless the source is not acknowledged in text.

30 Taped interview with Emily Smith, 1996. Further references to this interview will not be footnoted unless the source is not acknowledged in the text.

31 *Regina Leader-Post*, February 25, 1938

32 Telephone conversation with Michael Cobden, October 13, 1997

33 Telephone interview with Michael Cobden, 1996

34 "Tried and True", *The Toronto Sun*, September 19, 1978.

35 Brian Swarbrick, "'Just Plain True' Davidson is Ready to Begin a New Career at Age 70," *The Toronto Star*, March 13, 1971

36 Doris Pennington, *Agnes MacPhail: Reformer, Canada's First Female M.P.*, (Simon & Pierre: Toronto), 1989, p. 20

37 True Davidson, *The Golden Strings*, (Griffin House: Toronto), 1973.

38 A.M. Stephen, "Another B.C. Poet," *The Province*, Vancouver, February 9, 1932.

39 *Regina Leader-Post*, February 25, 1938

40 Resume headed "Memorandum regarding True Davidson," 1930, Archives and Special Collections, York University, 1978–004/08.

41 True Davidson, column published in *The Toronto Sun*, date unknown, from the collection of Nina Roberts.

42 *The Canadian Encyclopedia*, Second Edition, (Hurtig Publishers: Edmonton), 1988, p. 377

43 Website, http://www.net.gull-lake.sk.ca:80/town/clubs/cgit/cgit.htm

44 Warren Gerard, "True Davidson, Monarch of all East York," *The Globe Magazine*, March 13, 1971.

45 David Vienneau, "Last salute to True, the people's champion," *The Toronto Star*, September 22, 1978.

46 Letter of reference from Margaret E.T. Addison, Dean of Women, Victoria College, Toronto, March 24, 1922, Archives and Special Collections, York University, 1978–004/11.

47 Letter of reference from C.E. Augery, Registrar and Associate Professor of English, Victoria College, Toronto, March 25, 1922, Archives and Special Collections, York University, 1978–004/11

48 *Torontoniensis*, 1921, p. 65

49 Warren Gerard, "True Davidson, Monarch of all East York, *The Globe Magazine*, March 13, 1971.

50 Clara Thomas, *A Memoir of True*, unpublished paper

51 Doris Pennington, *Agnes Macphail: Reformer, Canada's First Female M.P.*, (Simon & Pierre: Toronto), 1989, p. 17

52 Warren Gerard, "True Davidson, Monarch of all East York," *The Globe Magazine*, March 13, 1971.

53 Clara Thomas, *A Memoir of True*, unpublished paper. With the gracious permission of its author.

54 Archives and Special Collections, York University, 1978–004/03

55 Resume headed "Memorandum Regarding True Davidson," Archives and Special Collections, York University, 1978–004/08.

56 Ibid

57 Letters from the Office and the Recording Dean, Bryn Mawr College, Pennsylvania, April 14, 1925 and April 30, 1925, Archives and Special Collections, York University, 1978–004/11.

58 United Church of Canada/Victoria University, United Church of Canada, "Obituary—Rev. J.W. Davidson, B.A., B.D.," Hamilton Conference, Minutes, 1941.

CHAPTER 2 THE DENT YEARS 1926–1930

1 Taped interview with Charlotte Maher, 1997

1 Handout from the 1966 election campaign, "Who Is True Davidson?", Archives and Special Collections, York University, 1978–004

3 Resume titled "Memorandum Regarding True Davidson", 1930, Archives and Special Collections, York University, 1978–004/08

4 Warren Gerard, "True Davidson, Monarch of all East York," *The Globe Magazine*, March 13, 1971

5 Letter from D. McIntyre to Mr. Henry Button, December 16, 1927, Archives and Special Collections, York University, 1978–004/08

6 Taped interview with Reeta Wright, 1996. Further references to this interview will not be footnoted unless the source is not identified in the text.

7 Archives and Special Collections, York University, 1978–04/03

8 Card from the President's Office, The MacMillan Company of Canada Limited Publishers, November 28th, 1928, signed "H.S.E.", Archives and Special Collections, York University, 1978–004/03

9 Book review column by True Davidson, *The Business Woman*, August 1930, Archives and Special Collections, York University, 1978–004/03

10 Newspaper clipping, ca. 1928, "Its Literature Can Do Much to Benefit Canada", unidentified Barrie newspaper, Archives and Special Collections, York University, 1978–004/03

11 Ibid

12 True Davidson, "The Philistine Years," *The New Outlook*, December 31, 1930, Archives and Special Collections, York University, 1978–004/03

13 *The Canadian Encyclopedia*, Second Edition, (Hurtig Publishers: Edmonton), 1988, p. 377

14 Ibid, p. 2026

15 Election flyer, 1966, "Who is True Davidson?", Archives and Special Collections, York University, 1978–004/07

16 Resume, "Memorandum Regarding True Davidson", 1930, Archives and Special Collections, York University, 1978–004/08

17 Ibid

CHAPTER 3 A STRUGGLING WRITER 1930–1931

1 *Chatelaine*, September 1931.

2 Letter of reference, written by Margaret T. MacKenzie (Mrs. Norman MacKenzie), Convenor of the Vocational Committee, Canadian Federation of University Women, July 30, 1931, Archives and Special Collections, York University, 1978–004/08.

3 Letter to True Davidson from the members of the Vocational Committee, Canadian Federation of University Women, January 14, 1932, Archives and Special Collections, York University, 1978–004/08

4 True Davidson, *The Golden Strings*, (Griffin House: Toronto), 1973, p. 121

5 Newspaper clipping, paper and date unknown, headlined "Trinity of Interests Election Hold Attention," Archives and Special Collections, York University, 1978/004–3B

6 Ibid

7 True Davidson, "True As You Live," *The East York Times*, undated newspaper clipping, ca. 1975, Archives and Special Collections, York University, 1978–004/03

8 A.M. Stephen, "Another B.C. Poet/Muses of The Modern Day and Other Days—By True Davidson—J.M. Dent & Sons Ltd.," *The Vancouver Province*, February 9, 1932

9 E.J. Pratt, "Muses of the Modern Day," *The Canadian Student*, date unknown, clipping found in Archives and Special Collections, York University, 1978–004/04

10 Newspaper clipping of a poem in a scrapbook kept by T. Davidson. "Double Entry," by Frances Bragan Richman, date unknown, Archives and Special Collections, York University, 1978–004/01

11 Archives and Special Collections, York University, 1978–004/04

12 Archives and Special Collections, York University, 1978–004/02A

13 Archives and Special Collections, York University, 1978–004/10B

14 Clara Thomas, *A Memoir of True*, unpublished paper
15 Archives and Special Collections, York University, 1978–004/04
16 Archives and Special Collections, York University, 1978–004/10B
17 Newspaper clipping, paper unidentified, Archives and Special Collections, York University, 1978–004/02A
18 Terry Crowley, *Agnes MacPhail and the Politics of Equality,* (J. Lorimer: Toronto), 1990, p. 93
19 Letter from Anna N. Sissons to True Davidson, Archives and Special Collections, York University, 1978–004/08
20 Draft for a column in the *Toronto Sun*, Archives and Special Collections, York University, 1978–004/02B
21 Lewis Levendel, "East York's True Davidson, 70, Wants to Be MPP," *The Toronto Star*, February 17, 1971
22 Walter Young, *The Anatomy of a Party: the national CCF 1932–61,* (University of Toronto Press: Toronto), 1969, p. 54
23 Ibid, p. 58
24 True Davidson, *The Golden Strings,* (Griffin House: Toronto), 1973, p. 140
25 Archives and Special Collections, York University, 1978–004/04A
26 True Davidson, *The Golden Strings*, (Griffin House: Toronto), 1973, p. 110

CHAPTER 4   WORKING FOR PERKINS BULL 1931–1938

1 "What Was to Be 50-Page History Grows Into Many Volumes," *Regina-Leader-Post*, February 25, 1938
2 Donald Jones, "Death of an heiress shook Rosedale," *The Toronto Star*, April 12, 1980
3 "What Was to Be 50-Page History Grows Into Many Volumes," *Regina Leader-Post*, February 25, 1938
4 Draft article for the Soroptomist Club 17b, Archives and Special Collections, York University, 1978–004/02
5 Ibid
6 "What Was To Be 50-Page History Grows Into Many Volumes," *Regina Leader-Post*, February 25, 1938
7 Draft article for the Soroptomist Club 17b, Archives and Special Collections, York University, 1978–004/02
8 Ibid
9 Taped interview with Harry Evans. Further references to this interview will not be footnoted unless the source is not identified in the text.
10 Letter to author from Garfield Evans, Oct. 16, 1996.
11 Warren Gerrard, "True Davidson, Monarch of all East York," *The Globe Magazine*, March 13, 1971
12 Donald Jones, "Death of an heiress.shook Rosedale," *The Toronto Star*, April 12, 1980
13 "Bull Tells How Mrs. Sidley Lavished Gifts on Friends," *Toronto Daily Star*, July 22, 1938
14 Letter from W. Perkins Bull to H.E. Sampson, Esq., K.C., February 21, 1938, Archives and Special Collections, York University, 1978–004/02

15 Warren Gerard, "True Davidson, Monarch of all East York," *The Globe Magazine*, March 13, 1971
16 Lucy Booth Martyn, *Aristocratic Toronto: 19th Century Grandeur*, (Gage Publishing Ltd.: Toronto), p. 164–170
17 Ibid
18 Donald Jones, "Death of an heiress shook Rosedale," *The Toronto Star*, April 5, 1980
19 "What Was To Be 50-Page Peel History Grows Into Many Volumes," *Regina Leader-Post*, February 25, 1938
20 Donald Jones, "Death of an heiress shook Rosedale," *The Toronto Star*, April 5, 1980
21 Lucy Booth Martyn, *Aristocratic Toronto: 19th Century Grandeur*, (Gage Publishing Ltd.: Toronto), p. 164–170
22 Ibid
23 "Bull Doesn't Know Sidley Gift Amount," *Toronto Daily Star*, July 15, 1938
24 Lucy Booth Martyn, *Aristocratic Toronto: 19th Century Grandeur*, (Gage Publishing Ltd.: Toronto), p. 166–170
25 Ibid
26 "History of U.E.L. Families Traced By Perkins Bull," *Regina Daily Star*, March 9, 1938
27 Ibid
28 Archives and Special Collections, York University, 1978–004/06B
29 Will Produce Play By Canadian Girl," *The Toronto Star*, December 1, 1934
30 Newspaper clipping, "ALL THE RIVERS/New Three-Act Canadian Play/ Makes Favorable Impression," Archives and Special Collections, York Uni-versity, 1978–004/02
31 Newspaper clipping, "Art of Drama Most Human/"Head Winds" Lauded as "Home-Made and Home-Grown," *The Telegram*, date missing, Archives and Special Collections, York University, 1978–004/02A
32 "Bull Tells How Mrs. Sidley Lavished Gifts on Friends," *Toronto Daily Star*, July 22, 1938
33 "Perkins Bull Says Stopping Of Cheques 'Bit of Nuisance,'" *Toronto Daily Star*, July 21, 1938
34 "Bull Tells How Mrs. Sidley Lavished Gifts on Friends," *Toronto Daily Star*, July 22, 1938
35 "May Fight Return of Sidley Body Here," *The Toronto Daily Star*, July 27, 1938

CHAPTER 5 TRAGEDY AND THE STREETSVILLE YEARS 1938–1947

1 Warren Gerard, "True Davidson, Monarch of All East York", *The Globe Magazine*, March 13, 1971
2 Ibid
3 New Year's Greeting Card, December 25, 1941, Archives and Special Collections, York University, 1978–004/02B
4 Letter to author from Garfield Evans, September 8, 1996.
5 Ibid
6 Ibid
7 Letter to author from Joan I. Moore, September 16, 1996

8   *The Conservator*, April 24, 1941, p. 2

9   *The Streetsville Review*, April 24, 1941

10 Warren Gerard, "True Davidson, Monarch of all East York," *The Globe Magazine*, March 13, 1971

11 Letter to author from Garfield Evans, September 8, 1996

12 Archives and Special Collections, York University, 1978–004/02A

13 Letter to author from Joan I. Moore, September 16, 1996

14 George Starbuck Galbraith, clipping of poem, source unidentified, Archives and Special Collections, York University, 1978–004/01B

15 True Davidson, "The City," short story published in *The New Outlook*, ca. 1941, Archives and Special Collections, York University, 1978–004/03

16 True Davidson, *The Golden Strings*, (Griffin House: Toronto), 1973

CHAPTER 6 BEGINNING A NEW LIFE IN EAST YORK 1947–1958

1   Warren Gerard, "True Davidson, Monarch of All East York," *The Globe Magazine*, March 13, 1971

2   Ibid

3   "True Davidson, Dedicated First Mayor of East York dies at 77," *The Toronto Star*, September 18, 1978

4   Newspaper clipping, " 'Only Had Year to Live,' So True Entered Politics," name of paper missing, February 14, 1968, Archives & Special Collections, York University, 1978–004/11B

5   Letter to author from Gord Hazlett, November 27, 1996

6   Unidentified and undated newspaper clipping in East York Library scrapbook about True Davidson, "Friendly People Made True Stay"

7   Warren Gerard, "True Davidson, Monarch of All East York," *The Globe Magazine*, March 13, 1971

8   Lewis Levendel, "East York's True Davidson, 70, Wants To Be MPP," *The Toronto Star*, February 17, 1971

9   Newspaper clipping, paper unidentified, " 'Only Had Year Live,' So True Entered Politics," February 14, 1968, Archives and Special Collections, York University, 1978–004/11B

10 Telephone interview with Jack Christie. Further references will not be foot noted unless source is unidentified in text.

11 True Davidson, *The Golden Strings*, (Griffin House: Toronto), 1973

12 Doris Pennington, *Agnes Macphail: Reformer, Canada's First Female M.P.*, (Simon & Pierre: Toronto), 1989

13 "True Davidson, Dedicated First Mayor of East York Dies at 77," *The Toronto Star*, September 18, 1978

14 Newspaper clipping, paper unidentified, " 'Only Had Year to Live,' So True Entered Politics," February 14, 1968, Archives and Special Collections, York University, 1978–004/11B

15 Lewis Levendel, "East York's True Davidson, 70, Wants To Be MPP," *The Toronto Star*, February 17, 1971

16 Letter to Emily Smith from True Davidson, August 3, 1950, collection of Mrs. Smith

17 Election handout, "Who Is True Davidson?", 1966, Archives and Special Collections, York University, 1978–004/02A

18 Tribute to True Davidson, Delivered by Dalton A. Morrison, Director of Education, East York Board of Education, at True Davidson's funeral, Woodbine United Church, September 21, 1978, copy in author's collection

19 Speech given to the Kiwanis when she became their first Citizen of the Year, ca. 1972, Archives and Special Collections, York University, 1978–004/04

20 "True Davidson, Dedicated First Mayor of East York dies at 77," *The Toronto Star*, September 19, 1978

21 "Tried and True," *The Toronto Sun*, September 19, 1978

22 Letter to Emily Smith from True Davidson, August 3, 1950, author has a copy

23 Speech to the East York Kiwanis, ca. 1972, Archives and Special Collections, York University, 1978–004/04

24 Ibid

25 Tribute to True Davidson, delivered by Dalton A. Morrison, Director of Education, East York Board of Education, at True Davidson's funeral, Woodbine United Church, September 21, 1978, author has a copy

26 Telephone interview with Helen Juhola

27 *The Cosburn Comet*, 1952–53, Archives and Special Collections, York University, 1978–004/03A

28 Newspaper clipping, paper unidentified, "Candidate Cites Maturity of Canada's Personality," December 7, ca. 1948, Archives and Special Collections, York University, 1978–004/04

29 Flyer, "'What Every Canadian Should Know' by True Davidson, M.A., ten lectures, Monday evenings, 8 p.m., October 10 to December 12 inclusive," Archives and Special Collections, York University, 1978–004/03B

30 Lewid Levendel, "East York's True Davidson, 70, Wants To Be MPP," *The Toronto Star*, February 17, 1971

31 *The Golden Years of East York*, edited from notes researched by True Davidson, (Centennial College Press: Toronto), 1976, p. 75

32 *The Golden Years of East York*, (Centennial College: Toronto), 1976, p. 80

33 Ibid

34 Letter to author from Tom Edwards, September 18, 1996, author's files

35 Ibid

36 Terry Crowley, *Agnes MacPhail and the Politics of Equality*, (J. Lorimer: Toronto), 1990

37 Warren Gerard, "True Davidson, Monarch of all East York," *The Globe Magazine*, March 13, 1971

38 Walter D. Young, *The anatomy of a party: the national CCF 1932–61*, (University of Toronto Press: Toronto), 1969, p. 289

39 Undated part of a page from the *York East CCF News*, Vol. II, No. 2, Archives and Special Collections, York University, 1978–004/03A

40 "Tried and True," *The Toronto Sun*, September 19, 1978

41 Taped interview with Nina Roberts

42 Martin Lipset, *Agrarian Socialism*, quoted in Kenneth McNaught, *A Prophet in Politics*, (University of Toronto Press: Toronto), 1959, p. 267

43 Walter D. Young, *The anatomy of a party: the national CCF 1932–1961*, (University of Toronto Press: Toronto), 1969, p. 291–292

44 "True Davidson, Mayor of East York for 11 Years," *The Globe and Mail*, September 19, 1978

45 Warren Gerard, "True Davidson, Monarch of all East York," *The Globe Magazine*, March 13, 1971

46 "True Davidson, Dedicated First Mayor of East York Dies at 77," *The Toronto Star*, September 18, 1971

47 True Davidson, *The Golden Strings*, (Griffin House: Toronto), 1973, p. 69

48 Lewis Levendel, "East York's True Davidson, 70, Wants to Be MPP," *The Toronto Star*, February 17, 1971

49 Newspaper clipping, paper and date missing, Archives and Special Collections, York University, 1978–004/01

50 True Davidson, "True Davidson says we waste too much," *The Toronto Star*, July 8, 1974

51 "True knows what its like to be vainly seeking work," *The Toronto Star*, December 3, 1971

52 Taped interview with Willis Blair. Will not be footnoted again unless source is unidentified in text.

53 Letter to Emily Smith from True Davidson, August 3, 1950, author has a copy

54 Mr. Powers, "Secrets of Charm," *Toronto Daily Star*, March 24, 1949

55 *The Hillfield Piglet*, ca. 1954–55, Archives and Special Collections, York University, 1978–004/01

56 "True Says Education Institute Useless,"*The Toronto Star*, April 14, 1971

CHAPTER 7 THE GHOST AND MISS DAVIDSON 1958–1962

1 Unidentified and undated newspaper clipping, "True Davidson Tops Polls in First Try," Archives and Special Collections, York University, 1978–004/06B

2 Speech to the Kiwanis, ca. 1972, Archives and Special Collections, York University, 1978–004

3 "True Davidson Calls for Sale of Twp. Land," *East Toronto Weekly and East York Times*, October 20, 1959

4 "True Hands Over Deeds," *East Toronto Weekly and East York Times*, November 30, 1961

5 Speech to Kiwanis Club, ca. 1972, Archives and Special Collections, York University, 1978–004

6 Election flyer resume, 1960, Archives and Special Collections, York University, 1978–004

7 Warren Gerard, "True Davidson, Monarch of all East York," *The Globe Magazine*, March 13, 1971

8 Campaign resume, 1960, Archives and Special Collections, York University, 1978–004

9 Full-page advertisement, "For Reeve—December 5," *East York Times-Supplement*, November 30, 1960

10 Archives and Special Collections, York University, 1978–004/01

11 Speech to the East York Kiwanis, ca. 1972, Archives and Special Collections, York University, 1978–004

12 "True Davidson looks back on 24 years in politics," *The Toronto Star*, December 18, 1972

13 "First Woman Reeve," *Toronto Daily Star*, December 3, 1960

14 Text for a speech given to the Association of Ontario Mayors and Reeves, June 27, 1962, Archives and Special Collections, York University, 1978–004/06A

15 *The Leaside Villager*, Friday, Nov. 27, 1981

16 Illuminated address from York University, June 8, 1978, Archives and Special Collections, York University, displayed in True Davidson reading room

17 Christmas card from True Davidson, 1964, Archives and Special Collections, York University, 1978–004

18 "Reeve True Davidson Reports," *The East York Times*, June 1961

19 Colin Davies, unidentified and undated newspaper clipping, "69,373 in Miss True's family, They're as Close as her Telephone," Archives and Special Collections, York University, 1978–004/11B

20 "For Reeve—On December 3rd," *East York Times*, November 28, 1962

21 Text for a speech to the Association of Mayors and Reeves, June 27, 1962, Archives and Special Collections, York University, 1978–004/06A

22 "She put East York on the map," *The Globe and Mail*, September 19, 1978

23 Brian Swarbrick, "Just Plain True' Davidson Is Ready To Begin A Brand New Career at 70," *The Toronto Star*, March 13, 1971

24 True Davidson, "True As You Live," *The East York News*, undated clipping, ca. 1975, Archives and Special Collections, York University, 1978–004/03

25 "True knows what its like to be vainly seeking work," *The Toronto Star*, December 3, 1971

26 Eloise Wilkinson, "East York's 'Chief' Believes in Her Ability," *The Windsor Star*, May 13, 1970

27 Dick Beddoes, "The True test was integrity," *The Globe and Mail*, September 19, 1978

28 Brian Swarbrick, "'Just Plain True' Davidson is Ready To Begin a Brand New Career at 70," *The Toronto Star*, March 13, 1971

29 Robert MacDonald, "East York Hopefuls Cry Foul At True's Huge Margin," *The Toronto Telegram*, December 2, 1969

30 Warren Gerard, "True Davidson, Monarch of all East York," *The Globe Magazine*, March 13, 1971

31 John Dowling, "True was always true to herself," *The Toronto Sun*, September 19, 1978

32 "True Davidson," *The Toronto Star*, September 18, 1978

33 Brian Swarbrick, "Just Plain True' Davidson Is Ready To Begin A Brand New Career At 70," *The Toronto Star*, March 13, 1971

34 Clara Thomas, *A Memoir of True*, unpublished paper

35 Poem clipped from an unidentified and undated newspaper, Archives and Special Collections, York University, 1978–004/01B

CHAPTER 8 METRO COUNCIL AND
THE FIGHT AGAINST AMALGAMATION 1962–1966

1 Robertson Cochrane, "First Woman Reeve," *The Toronto Star*, December 3, 1960

2　Dick Beddoes, "The True test was integrity," *The Globe and Mail*, September 19, 1978

3　Text for a speech for the Association of Ontario Mayors and Reeves, June 27, 1962, Archives and Special Collections, York University, 1978–004/06A

4　True Davidson, *The Golden Strings*, (Griffin House:Toronto), 1973, p. 56–58

5　Dick Beddoes, "The True test was integrity," *The Globe and Mail*, September 19, 1978

6　Letter to author from Joan I. Moore, September 16, 1996

7　"True Davidson, Mayor of East York for 11 Years," *The Globe and Mail*, September 19, 1978

8　"True Davidson Dead At 77," *The Toronto Star*, September 18, 1978

9　Ian Urquhart, "True Davidson is thinking of quitting," *The Toronto Star*, September 1, 1972

10　Robert Douglas, "Hotel throws a party for 300 cabbies," *The Toronto Star*, March 30, 1972

11　"True Davidson urges Metro to limit population growth," *The Toronto Star*, January 22, 1972

12　Newspaper clipping from unidentified and undated paper, "True Says She's Tired of Old World Feuds Brought Over Here," Archives and Special Collections, York University, 1978–004/11B

13　"Metro Councillors Accuse True of Electioneering," *The Toronto Star*, May 19, 1971

14　"Criminals on Roads Assailed By True," *The Toronto Star*, undated clipping, Archives and Special Collections, York University, 1978–004/11B

15　"Metro mayors are cool to Eglinton subway plan," *The Toronto Star*, October 27, 1971

16　Warren Gerard, "True Davidson, Monarch of All East York," *The Globe Magazine*, March 13, 1971

17　Letter to author from June Callwood, September 24, 1997

18　Unidentified and undated newspaper clipping, "True Resigns from Planning Council," Archives and Special Collections, York University, 1978 –004/11B

19　President's Report to the Association of Mayors and Reeves of Ontario, 1969, Archives and Special Collections, York University, 1978–004/06A

20　Unidentified newspaper clipping, " 'Only Had Year to Live', So True Entered Politics," February 15, 1968, Archives and Special Collections, York University, 1978–004/11B

21　Text for a speech for the Association of Ontario Mayors and Reeves, June 27, 1962, Archives and Special Collections, York University, 1978–004/06A

22　"Spadina Rejection 'Endangers' Metro's Self-Rule," *The Toronto Star*, June 4, 1971

23　Dick Beddoes, "The True test was integrity," *The Globe and Mail*, September 19, 1978

24　"True Davidson", *The Toronto Star*, September 18, 1978

25　Notes from the East York brief and True Davidson's personal summary report to the Goldenberg Commission, 1964, Archives and Special Collections, York University, 1978–004/05

26　Text of a talk given by Doris Tucker at Central Park Lodge, November 1990, author has a copy

27 Election flyer, "Who Is True Davidson?", Archives and Special Collections, York University, 1978–004

28 "The Voters Say," *The Toronto Star*, December 2, 1966

29 "True Davidson," *The Globe and Mail*, September 19, 1978

30 "The Voters Say," *The Toronto Star*, December 2, 1960

31 Unidentified newspaper clipping, " 'Only Had Year to Live,' So True Entered Politics," February 14, 1968, Archives and Special Collections, York University, 1978–004/11B

32 True Davidson, "Go to it, Hazel!," *The Toronto Sun*, March 27, 1973

CHAPTER 9 A WOMAN IN POLITICS

1 Handwitten copies of various quotations, Archives and Special Collections, York University 1978–004/04A

2 True Davidson, *The Golden Strings,* (Griffin House: Toronto), 1973, p. 64–65

3 "The Voters Say," *The Toronto Star*, December 2, 1966

4 Letter to author from Jim Lister, September 23, 1996

5 Unidentified newspaper clipping, "Only Had Year to Live," So True Entered Politics," February 14, 1968, Archives and Special Collections, York University, 1978–004/11B

6 Eloise Wilkinson, "East York's Chief Believes In Her Ability," *The Windsor Star*, May 13, 1970

7 True Davidson, *The Golden Strings,* (Griffin House: Toronto), 1973, p. 35–36

8 Archives and Special Collections, York University, 1978–004/06B

9 Dalton Morrison, Director of Education, "Tribute to True Davidson, delivered at True's funeral," September 21, 1978

10 "True Davidson pointed the way," *The Toronto Star*, September 19, 1978

11 "True Davidson," *The Toronto Star*, September 18, 1978

12 Unidentified newspaper clipping, February 14, 1968, Archives & Special Collections, York University, 1978–004

13 Draft text for her column in *The Toronto Sun*, Archives and Special Collections, York University, 1978–004/05

14 True Davidson, "The moving finger," *The Toronto Sun*, March 8, 1973

15 Ian Urquhart, "True Davidson is thinking of quitting," *The Toronto Star*, September 1, 1972

16 Elizabeth Smith, "True Plans Book On the Women Who Built Canada," *The Spectator*, April 24, 1974

17 Author's recollection of a conversation with Jeanne Hughes at a dinner, 1996

18 "Reflections in the Mirror," *The Mirror*, July 14, 1967

19 Election card, Archives and Special Collections, York University, 1978–004/05

20 Eloise Wilkinson, "East York's Chief Believes In Her Ability," *The Windsor Star*, May 13, 1970

21 True Davidson, "Margaret Campbell," *The Toronto Sun*, March 13, 1973

22 Ross Howard, "True has her eye on Queen's Park," *The Toronto Telegram*, February 16, 1971

23 Warren Gerard, "True Davidson, Monarch of all East York," *The Globe Magazine*, March 13, 1971

24 Dalton Morrison, "Tribute to True Davidson at her funeral," September 21, 1978

25 Draft text for her column in *The Toronto Sun*, Archives and Special Collections, York University, 1978–004/05

26 "True Davidson," *The Globe and Mail*, September 19, 1978

27 True Davidson, "True As You Live," *The East York News*, undated clipping, ca. 1975, Archives and Special Collections, York University, 1978–004/03

28 Letter to author from June Callwood, September 24, 1997

29 Lewis Levendel, "East York's True Davidson, 70, Wants to Be MPP," *The Toronto Star*, February 17, 1971

30 Flyer, Archives and Special Collections, York University, 1978–004/05

31 Dick Beddoes, "The True test was integrity," *The Globe and Mail*, September 19, 1978

32 Letter to author from June Callwood, September 24, 1997

33 Unidentified newspaper clipping, " 'Only Had Year To Live,' So True Entered Politics," February 14, 1968

34 Wendy Dey, "Fighting-trim' True wins her last race," *Toronto Daily Star*, December 2, 1969

35 Eloise Wilkinson, "East York's Chief Believes in Her Ability," *The Windsor Star*, May 13, 1970

36 Clara Thomas, *A Memoir of True*, unpublished paper.

37 Ibid

38 Citation, on wall of True Davidson Reading Room, York University

CHAPTER 10 MAYOR OF EAST YORK 1967–1972

1 Text of a talk given by Doris Tucker at Central Park Lodge, November 1990, author has a copy

2 Letter to author from Peter Worthington, October 4, 1997

3 Conversation with Michael Cobden, October 13, 1997

4 Ibid

5 Text for a speech to the East York Kiwanis, ca. 1972, Archives and Special Collections, York University, 1978–004/04

6 Outline of plans for the "East York Centennial Project," Archives and Special Collections, York University, 1978–004

7 "Ghost of John Simcoe was Late and True Davidson was Annoyed," *The Toronto Star*, August 3, 1971

8 E-mail to author from Mary Barnstaple, December 27, 1996

9 Christmas Card, 1965, Archives and Special Collections, York University, 1978–004/03

10 Speech to the East York Kiwanis, ca. 1972, Archives and Special Collections, York University, 1978–004/04

11 President's Report to the Association of Mayors and Reeves, 1969, Archives and Special Collections, York University, 1978–004/06A

12 True Davidson, "True As You Live," *The East York Times*, ca. 1975, clipping in the collection of Archives and Special Collections, York University, 1978–04/03

13 Telephone interview with Alan Redway, September 21, 1997

14 Ibid

15 Speech given by True about her attendance at the conference, "The Centennial Study and Trustee Programme on Metro Problems—August 16, 1967," Archives and Special Collections, York University, 1978–004/01B

16 Ibid

17 Letter to author from Joyce Crook, December 2, 1996. True was not alone in her advocacy of the Red Ensign as Ontario's flag.

18 Clara Thomas, *A Memoir of True*, unpublished paper

19 Warren Gerard, "True Davidson, Monarch of all East York," *The Globe Magazine*, March 13, 1971

20 Letter from True Davidson to Emily Smith, 1950, author has a copy

21 Conversation with Michael Cobden, October 13, 1997

22 President's Report to the Association of Mayors and Reeves of Ontario, 1969, Archives and Special Collections, York University, 1978–004/06A

CHAPTER 11 THE GRANDMOTHER OF EAST YORK 1969–1972

1 Edna Hampton, "Test Nearing Of East Yorkers' Loyalty To Their Mayor of Nine Years," *The Globe and Mail*, November 8, 1969

2 "Fighting-Trim' True Wins Her Last Race," *Toronto Daily Star*, December 2, 1969

3 Robert MacDonald, "East York Hopefuls Cry Foul At True's Huge Margin," *The Toronto Telegram*, December 2, 1969

4 Warren Gerard, "True Davidson, Monarch of all East York," *The Globe Magazine*, March 13, 1971

5 Ibid

6 "Centennial in East York," *The East End Express*, September 15, 1971

7 Edna Hampton, "Test Is Nearing Of East Yorkers' Loyalty To Their Mayor of Nine Years," *The Globe and Mail,* November 8, 1969

8 Conversation with Michael Cobden, October 13, 1997

9 Warren Gerard, "True Davidson, Mayor of all East York," *The Globe Magazine*, March 13, 1971

10 Conversation with Michael Cobden, October 13, 1997

11 Ibid

12 True Davidson, "Gift of God," *The Toronto Sun*, undated clipping from the collection of Nina Roberts, ca. 1977

13 Muriel Tozer declined to be interviewed.

14 Letter to author from June Callwood, September 24, 1997

15 "True To The Rescue In Hot Water Hassle," *The Toronto Star*, September 20, 1971

16 Letter to Eleanor Darke from Jim Lister, September 23, 1996

17 Ibid

18 Ross Howard, "True has her eye on Queen's Park," *The Toronto Telegram*, February 16, 1971

19 Robert Sutton, "rival views True as another thorny Shulman," *The Toronto Telegram*, February 17, 1971

20 Ross Howard, "True has her eye on Queen's Park," *The Toronto Telegram*, February 16, 1971

21 Lewis Levendel, "East York's True Davidson, 70, Wants To Be MPP," *The Toronto Star*, February 17, 1971

22 Brian Swarbrick, "Just Plain True' Davidson Is Ready To Begin A Brand New Career at 70," *The Toronto Star*, March 13, 1971

23 "True Gets Half-Fare Card for TTC," *The Toronto Star*, March 24, 1971

24 Gerald McDuff, "True And 300 Friends Have Fun At Her 70th Birthday Bash," *The Toronto Star*, April 20, 1971

25 Election flyer, Archives and Special Collections, York University, 1978–004/05

26 "Had no chance," True defeated in East York," *The Toronto Star*, October 22, 1971

27 "'Just Plain True' Davidson Is Ready To Begin A Brand New Career At 70," *The Toronto Star*, March 13, 1971

28 Ian Urquhart, "True Davidson is thinking of quitting," *The Toronto Star*, September 1, 1972

29 Ibid

30 True Davidson, "True As You Live," *The East York News*, undated clipping, ca. 1975, Archives and Special Collections, York University, 1978–004/03

CHAPTER 12 AN ELDER OF THE TRIBE 1972–1978

1 Elizabeth Smith, "True Plans Book On The Women Who Built Canada," *The Spectator*, April 24, 1974

2 "Tried and True," *The Toronto Sun*, September 19, 1978

3 True Davidson, "We are to blame, not government," *The Toronto Sun*, March 20, 1973

4 Letter to author from Frank Russell, 1996

5 John Downing, "True was always true to herself," *The Toronto Sun*, September 19, 1978

6 True Davidson, "Who owns a child?", *The Toronto Sun*, March 6, 1973

7 True Davidson, "The moving finger," *The Toronto Sun*, March 8, 1973

8 True Davidson, "Who to blame?," *The Toronto Sun*, March 15, 1973

9 True Davidson, "We are to blame, not government," *The Toronto Sun*, March 20, 1973

10 Letter to author from Peter Worthington, October 4, 1997

11 Ibid

12 Elizabeth Smith, "True Plans Book On The Women Who Built Canada," *The Spectator,* April 24, 1974

13 True Davidson, "True As You Live," *The East York News*, undated newspaper clipping, ca. 1975, Archives and Special Collections, York University, 1978–004/03

14 Discussion with Helen Juhola, 1997

15 Elizabeth Smith, "True Plans Book On The Women Who Built Canada," *The Spectator*, April 24, 1974

16 True Davidson, *The Golden Strings*, (Griffin House: Toronto), 1973, p. 151

17 Elizabeth Smith, "True Plans Book On the Women Who Built Canada," *The Spectator*, April 24, 1974

18 Ibid, p. 6

19 Christmas card poem by True Davidson, ca. 1977, collection of Doris Tucker

20 Letter to E. Darke from Garfield Evans, September 8, 1996

21 Letter to True Davidson from Florence Deacon, July 1, 1973, Archives and Special Collections, York University, 1978–004/07

22 Letter to True Davidson from June Callwood, March 20, 1976, Archives and Special Collections, York University, 1978–004/07

23 Letter to True Davidson from the Hon. John Diefenbaker, ca. 1977, Archives and Special Collections, York University, 1978–004/07

24 Dan Proudfoot, "Sherlock's Popularity Is No Mystery," *The Sunday Sun*, December 28, 1975

25 "True Grit," *The Toronto Sun*, September 19, 1978

26 Clara Thomas, *A Memoir of True*, unpublished paper

27 Ibid

28 John Downing, "True was always true to herself," *The Toronto Sun*, September 19, 1978

29 Clara Thomas, *A Memoir of True*, an unpublished paper

30 "True Grit," *The Toronto Sun*, September 19, 1978

31 Letter to author from Peter Worthington, October 4, 1997

32 Rudyard Kiping, *The Two Jungle Books*. (Macmillan Publishing Co.: London), 1924 as quoted in *The Golden Strings*.

33 David Vienneau, "Last salute to True, the people's champion," *The Toronto Star*, September 21, 1978

34 Dalton A. Morrison, Director of Education, "Tribute to True Davidson at her funeral," September 21, 1978

35 Ibid

36 Text from the presentation of her honorary doctorate from York University, on display in the True Davidson Reading Rooms, Archives and Special Collections, York University

37 Letter to author from Peter Worthington, October 4, 1997

38 True's final poem, Archives and Special Collections, York University, 1978–004/11A

INDEX

ABOUT THE AUTHOR

It was during her tenure as Curator-Manager of the Todmorden Mills Historic site (1973–1984), that the author first met True Davidson.

Born in Scarborough, Ontario and a Don Mills resident since the age of three, Eleanor Darke has been fascinated by history from childhood, especially by the first-person stories and documents of those personally involved. In her pursuit of these interests the author obtained a B. A. (Honours) in Canadian history and English, Glendon College, York University. She also holds a certificate in Museum Studies, Ontario Museum Association.

Since 1995, Eleanor Darke has served as the Programme Officer, Toronto Historical Board (now called Heritage Toronto). Prior to which she was Site Manager at Mackenzie House, Toronto. She is the author of *A Mill Should Be Build Thereon*, published in 1995 by Natural Heritage.

The author is married to R. Fred Darke, photographer and video producer.